Shreveport
A Photographic Remembrance

Shreveport

A Photographic Remembrance, 1873–1949

Bailey Thomson and
Patricia L. Meador

Louisiana State University Press
Baton Rouge and London

Designer: Christopher Wilcox
Typeface: Times Roman
Typesetter: G & S Typesetters
Printer: Thomson Shore, Inc.
Binder: John Dekker & Sons, Inc.

Library of Congress Cataloging-in-Publication Data

Thomson, Bailey.
    Shreveport, a photographic remembrance, 1873–1949.

    Bibliography: p.
    Includes index.
    1. Shreveport (La.)—Description—Views.
2. Shreveport (La.)—Social life and customs—
Pictorial works.   I. Meador, Patricia L.
II. Title.
F379.S4T48   1986   976.3'99   86-14771
ISBN 0-8071-1311-5

For our mothers

Attie Kimbrell Thomson
Jessie Castle Meador

Contents

Acknowledgments

Several individuals and institutions deserve recognition and thanks for their contributions to this work. The Shreveport Bank and Trust Company provided encouragement and generous support all along the way, including an order for several thousand books in advance.

The staff of the LSUS Library, especially Malcolm Parker, the director, helped at every step of this project. Without his support, this book never could have come into being. Likewise, we benefited from the encouragement of the LSUS Archives Committee.

Dr. Charles T. Beaird, publisher of the Shreveport *Journal,* was a steady friend to this project. Through his family's newspaper, he provided financial assistance for our first photographic fair. He also offered invaluable advice on a wide range of questions. Stanley R. Tiner, editor of the *Journal,* always looked upon this project with enthusiasm. His interest in our region extends beyond reporting today's news to promoting an understanding of the historical currents that lie beneath it.

Along with Goodloe Stuck and Hubert Humphreys, Tom Ruffin read portions of this manuscript and made critical suggestions that improved its accuracy and in some cases its literary quality. All three are splendid local historians and cherished friends.

Laura Street and Tom Beistle, both members of the archives staff, worked faithfully to help secure and catalog the photographic collections. Others who deserve mention are Julia Adkins, Neil Johnson, and John Wilkins.

At the *Journal,* we want to thank Martha Fernandez, the librarian, for her help during the first fair. Jack Barham, director of the photographic department, gave us access to his extensive collections of negatives from the 1940s and then made prints for us. Ron Rice, who was then an artist at the paper, made useful suggestions on designing our book. Special thanks go to Annette Caramia, assistant editorial page editor, who filled in for her colleague when he was out chasing down photographs.

Other individuals and institutions who made significant contributions are noted in the Preface.

Shreveport

A Photographic Remembrance

Preface

One way to make the history of a region more accessible to its people is to collect letters, diaries, newspapers, government documents, and other written and printed materials that are the primary sources of historical writing. Another is to tape-record interviews with persons who have witnessed important events or who simply remember the old ways of living. These kinds of records belong in an archives, where scholars and students can use them.

Fortunately, Louisiana State University in Shreveport formally established such a repository for records of Northwest Louisiana in 1975, under the direction of my coauthor, Patricia Meador. Before then, Professor Hubert Humphreys and librarian Malcolm Parker had been collecting materials for several years. The holdings of the LSUS Archives continue to grow, as does the number of people who use them.

Still, one source of information largely eluded researchers: old photographs. We knew that professional photographers worked in the region as early as the 1870s. We suspected that amateurs had discovered the pleasures of photography by the 1890s, when improved technologies made snapshot cameras and films available.

Certain treasures already were in the archives. In 1968, for example, the university purchased from a private collector a remarkable group of 107 hand-tinted albumin photographs taken by R. B. Talfor in 1873. They documented the removal of the remaining logjams in the Red River by the United States Army Corps of Engineers. Only one other set of photographs from Talfor's negatives exists, and that one is in the Library of Congress.

Occasionally, a person brought photographs to the archives, or a donor included photographs in personal papers. Also, local historians, digging through trunks or old file cabinets, sometimes ran across historic photographs. Many more pictures would be required, however, for a fully representative photographic record of the history of Northwest Louisiana.

In 1980 the archives secured a grant from the Community Foundation of Shreveport-Bossier to establish a special photographic section. The money went toward purchasing a copy camera and darkroom equipment and toward training the staff at the archives in photographic preservation.

In 1982 the archives received a second grant—this one from the Louisiana Committee for the Humanities—to collect and exhibit historic photographs, and the Community Foundation provided some matching funds. With money from the grants and in partnership with the Shreveport *Journal,* the archives organized a Community Photographic Fair to be held in downtown Shreveport in November, 1982. People were invited to bring their old photographs and to tell about them. Volunteers recorded the information, and the staff made copies of the negatives. Many people donated their photographs. The fair drew some five hundred visitors, and for their enjoyment, the organizers presented a display of mounted photographs from the archives' existing collections and also a slide and sound show on Shreveport's history. As an incentive to participants, the *Journal* offered cash prizes for the best entries in several categories, along with a grand prize for the best in the show. In all, the fair brought the archives more than two thousand photographs, many of which appear in this book.

In 1983 the archives received another grant from the Louisiana Committee on the Humanities. This permitted Patricia Meador and her staff to organize a photographic fair for nearby Minden, Louisiana, in December of that year. Local sponsors were the Minden Bank and Trust Company and the Webster Parish Library. With this second fair, the archives reached far into Shreveport's hinterland for photographs on logging, cotton farming, rural schools, family life, and similar subjects. The staff added these images to the cataloged collections in the archives, which by that time held more than five thousand photographs.

Also, in October, 1983, the archives presented a new exhibit of seventy-five mounted prints. Ms. Meador and I had drawn inspiration for such exhibits—and also for the idea of going directly to the people for photographs—from a program called Vanishing Georgia. Under the sponsorship of the Georgia State Archives, the program sends teams of researchers and photographers around the state to gather photographs. Copies of negatives are collected and cataloged at the state archives in Atlanta, and from these negatives, exhibits are prepared.

There remained, however, a significant deficiency in our efforts. The great majority of people in the region have only limited access to the photographic collections of the LSUS Archives, and we needed a way to present to them at least the most outstanding photographs. Thus the idea for this book occurred to us. We also wanted to visit some major photographic repositories around the country and bring home any images of our region that we might find there.

To support this phase, we turned once more to the Community Foundation, our faithful benefactor. A new grant permitted us to secure the services of Thurmond Smith, whose photographic studio uses a combination of filters and other state-of-the-art techniques to turn faded images on copies of old negatives into sparkling prints. Meanwhile, Patricia Meador and I set about winnowing the essential photographs from the archives' collections.

We continued to search for additions. For example, in the National Archives and the Library of Congress in Washington, D.C., we came upon a number of priceless photographs, including four that Lewis Hine took in Shreveport in 1913. Hine described his works as "photo-interpretations." His thousands of photographs, taken all over the country, were powerful enough to help secure passage of child-labor laws. In Washington and also in the Louisiana State Library in Baton Rouge we found photographs of Northwest Louisiana in collections of the Works Progress Administration and other federal agencies. Documentary photographs, especially from the WPA collections, helped to shape the later development of photojournalism. More than mere illustrations, these photographs are subjective interpretations of their time.

One of our few disappointments was the relative scarcity of photographs that depict the lives of blacks in our region. For the most part, early professional photographers whose work survives left us images of whites. Here and there, one finds a few photographs that have blacks in them—and some of those are truly remarkable documents. For example, one shows black laborers laying bricks on Texas Street in Shreveport around 1898; another shows black voters lined up at the Caddo Parish Courthouse about 1894. A greater number of photographs of blacks exist from the 1920s and later decades, but not nearly as many as we had hoped. Our expectations soared at one point when we learned of a privately held collection of negatives that had been taken by a black photographer in Shreveport. Alas, the negatives had survived a fire, and some were damaged. None had any identification, and they were useless for our purposes.

We decided that the purpose of our book would be to illustrate with photographs a period of local history from 1873 to 1949. The archives' collections begin with photographs from the first date. The second date is for the most part arbitrary. Our goal is essentially documentary. In Shreveport, photojournalism, as opposed to the more conventional documentary styles, dates from the late 1940s, when young photographers such as Jack Barham and Langston McEachern began trying to capture the news on film for the local papers. Our book, by contrast, is more concerned with documenting everyday social conditions—how things looked and how people lived.

In considering how best to present the photographs, I turned for advice to Goodloe Stuck, who in 1980 helped me write *Historic Shreveport: A Guide*. He suggested that we should do more than simply identify the photographs. We needed to place the photographs in their historical context and also convey a broad sense of the region's history. This led me not only to published works on local history but also to the extensive primary sources that the archives' staff has gathered.

While I was doing the research and writing the text, Ms. Meador worked with Tom Beistle, the archives' staff photographer, and Thurmond Smith to secure the finest prints possible. Occasionally, this meant going back to the donor and borrowing the original photograph again to make a better copy of the negative. Ms. Meador also compiled the bibliography.

Our hope is that this book will reach a large audience and complement the good work on Northwest Louisiana that is being done at LSUS. The university's contributions include administration of the Pioneer Heritage Center, publication of the *North Louisiana Historical Association Journal*, and continuing research and courses on the history of the region. Meanwhile, scholars at other institutions, especially Louisiana Tech University, are pursuing similar activities, with the common purpose of learning more about Northwest Louisiana's history and culture. We hope this book will benefit everyone with an interest in the field.

BAILEY THOMSON

Part I

The Early City
and Its Hinterland

Shreve Town began in the 1830s as a business venture in a fashion typical of many towns that dotted the American West in the nineteenth century. From the beginning, the settlement had a good chance for success. It sat upon land high above the Red River. Nearby were fertile river bottoms, forests of pine and oak, and—though unknown until this century—deposits of oil and gas.

The decade of the 1830s witnessed the removal of the "Great Raft," a series of logjams stretching for some 160 miles above Natchitoches, and this feat made accessible an estimated 1.5 million acres of federal land.[1] As hordes of settlers descended upon the region, the town became the new head of steamboat traffic on the Red.

Because most antebellum roads were little more than improved Indian trails, the river served as a great highway for settlement and commerce, and boats plied streams and natural lakes to reach distant points.[2] The steamboat made commercial agriculture possible in these new lands, and not even the Panic of 1837 could suppress for long the fever to grow cotton.

Among the town's eight founders was Captain Henry Miller Shreve, a remarkably energetic figure of the Jacksonian period. Although he gave his name to the settlement, Shreve never established residence there. As federal superintendent of western rivers improvement, he led the expedition of men and vessels that removed the Raft from the Red River. The work lasted from 1833 to 1839. Earlier, he had developed the prototype of the shallow-hull steamboat and had invented a snagboat for clearing rivers of dangerous obstacles.

In May, 1836, Shreve joined a venture called the Shreve Town Company, whose leading partner was Angus McNeill. A few months earlier, McNeill had purchased rights to land that was desirable for a town site. For this, he had paid $5,000 to Larkin Edwards, whom the Caddo Indians had given 640 acres to be staked wherever he chose within their vast cession to the federal government. McNeill agreed to share ownership in the land with the investors who joined him in creating the Shreve Town Company. The site was along the river where two New Englanders named James Cane and William Bennett ran a trading post. The partnership of Bennett and Cane, in turn, became one of the seven

1. Hubert Davis Humphreys, "The 'Great Raft' of the Red River," in B. H. Gilley (ed.), *North Louisiana: Essays on the Region and Its History to 1865* (Ruston, La., 1984), 73.

2. Morgan Peoples, "Politics, Parties, and Politicians in Antebellum North Louisiana, 1812–1865," in Gilley (ed.), *North Louisiana*, 134–35.

stockholders in the new company. In 1837 the founders re-named their town Shreveport.[3]

The founders commemorated the Texas Revolution by naming several of the streets for its heroes: Crockett, Fannin, Travis, and Milam. The new town was eight streets wide and eight streets long—a gridiron pattern that was common in the West during the eighteenth and early nineteenth centuries. The gridiron was convenient for selling real estate, but it often ignored local topography. In Shreveport, for example, parts of several streets lay under Silver Lake, a body of water, now gone, that was the town's southern boundary.

In 1839 the Louisiana legislature incorporated the town and gave it a charter. It also designated Shreveport as the seat of justice for Caddo Parish, which had been created a year earlier. Many of the town's first structures sat on lots that were no more than clearings in the woods. In fact, one of the first ordinances provided for the "cutting out" of Commerce Street and the removal of stumps. In this raw setting, where ruffians and professional men alike went about armed, violence was common. The town's first mayor, John Sewall, died in a duel in 1840. Organized religion, meanwhile, was slow to arrive. There were no services until March 24, 1839, when Leonidas Polk, an Episcopal bishop, visited. He returned two years later to find that no other sermons had been preached in the town during his absence.[4]

Shreveport clung to life, even as logjams gradually re-formed upriver all the way to Arkansas and other towns arose to compete for the area's trade. One such settlement was nearby Coates' Bluff. In early 1837 Shreve eliminated its competition when he had his men cut a new channel for the river. He justified the action on the grounds that the new channel would be shorter. A more serious threat of competition came from Jefferson, Texas, a port some fifty miles away from the Red River. By plugging the river's channel, the logjams raised the level of lakes and bayous that drained into the river, which permitted boats to leave the river just above Shreveport and—traveling by way of Twelve Mile Bayou, Soda Lake, Caddo Lake, and Cypress Bayou—reach Jefferson. Along this route, several settlements grew up where farmers would take their cotton and await boats from Jefferson. The response from the Shreveport newspapers to this competition was to play up the perils of this tortuous water route to Jefferson.[5]

Promise of wealth from cotton drew settlers into the region, which had felt little of the French and Spanish influence during the colonial period. Josiah Gregg, who was a trader, explorer, and author, first visited Shreveport in 1841. In 1847 he included a description of the town in his journal: "It is at the highest point of Red R. below the present raft,

3. Fredricka Doll Gute and Katherine Brash Jeter, *Historical Profile: Shreveport, 1850* (Shreveport, 1982), 3–4; Edith S. McCall, *Conquering the Rivers: Henry Miller Shreve and the Navigation of America's Inland Waterways* (Baton Rouge, 1984), 215–18.

4. Gute and Jeter, *Historical Profile,* 4–5; *Shreveport Centennial, 1835–1935, Commemorating 100 Years of Progress* (Shreveport, 1967), 13, 17; Perry Anderson Snyder, "Shreveport, Louisiana, During the Civil War and Reconstruction (Ph.D. dissertation, Florida State University, 1979), 25–26.

5. Snyder, "Shreveport During the Civil War and Reconstruction," 21–24; J. Fair Hardin, "An Outline of Shreveport and Caddo Parish History," *Louisiana Historical Quarterly,* XVIII (1935), 92.

where a free outlet can be had westward. It therefore commands a very considerable trade from Texas, not only from that portion directly west, to the distance of 200 miles, but very frequently from 200 miles above."[6] Thus Shreveport became a trading center not only for Northwest Louisiana and eastern Texas but also for southeastern Arkansas and southwestern Oklahoma. Traveling over an oxcart highway, caravans reached the town even from Mexico.

In 1835 the Caddo Indians had signed a treaty with the federal government in which they agreed to sell their lands in the area for eighty thousand dollars and move westward. From the point of view of the whites, this removed yet another barrier to settlement, throwing open vast tracts of land for purchase from the government. But the Caddos remained until the 1840s. In 1838 a troop of soldiers from the Republic of Texas created an international incident when they chased a band of Caddos across the border and apprehended them in Shreveport. The Texans accused the Indians of marauding along the frontier and insisted that their captives surrender their guns and remain in Louisiana. Congress eventually mediated the quarrel after the United States annexed Texas in 1845.[7]

By 1850 the federal census showed a population of 1,728 people for Shreveport. There were several hotels, a number of saloons and gambling houses, and at least two brothels. Along with a courthouse and a jail, the town had two churches, one Methodist and one Baptist. The ethos of the frontier persisted. Albert Harris Leonard, whose family came to Shreveport by steamboat in 1849, recalled that as a boy he watched from the gallery of the Palmetto Hotel as an attacker knifed another man to death in the street.[8]

Shreveport's early economy depended upon cotton, which was the nation's chief export. Expansion of the textile industry in Great Britain stimulated demand, and farms and plantations in Northwest Louisiana generally could count on profitable prices. In turn, cotton production lent itself particularly well to slave labor. The census of 1860 reports 7,338 slaves in Caddo Parish and 490 slaveholders.[9] Slavery proved to be more difficult to regulate in the towns and cities than in the country. In cities and towns there were more opportunities for blacks to escape constant supervision.

Efforts to address this problem were reflected in Shreveport's local ordinances. For example, a slave found away from his proper domicile without a pass after 9 P.M. was to receive thirty-nine lashes. The same punishment applied for slaves caught "drinking or gaming." An exception was made for the Shreveport Ethiopian Band, which included the free black Norman Davis. Band members had permission to gather for practice provided they notified one of the town constables and were home by 11 P.M. Davis was one of twenty-one free Negroes that the census of 1850 lists for Shreveport. He was a mulatto barber who had bought ten

6. Tom Ruffin, "Josiah Grêgg and Shreveport During the 1840s," *North Louisiana Historical Association Journal*, IV (Summer, 1973), 145.

7. Tom Ruffin, "The Invasion of Shreveport," *Shreveport Magazine*, XXIV (July, 1969), 26, 34–38.

8. U.S. Bureau of the Census, *1980 Census of Population: Number of Inhabitants*, Volume I: *Characteristics of the Population* (Washington, D.C., 1983), 178; Gute and Jeter, *Historical Profile*, 4–8, 33, 41.

9. John D. Winters, "The Cotton Kingdom: Antebellum Northeast Louisiana," in Gilley (ed.), *North Louisiana*, 72.

acres along Texas Avenue in 1849, which he subdivided and sold in lots.[10]

As the frontier receded, the conservative Whig party gained followers in state and local politics, particularly among businessmen and planters. Unlike the Democrats, who insisted that the North yield to southern interests on the question of slavery, Whigs were nationalists who stressed trust and harmony between the sections. They favored internal improvements, protectionism, and a strong national financial system. In Shreveport, Whigs showed strength in the elections of 1844 and 1852, as the town supported the unsuccessful candidacies of Henry Clay and General Winfield Scott. The Whigs' nationalism could not withstand the sectional furor that arose over the Kansas-Nebraska Act in 1854, however, and the party collapsed. Many old Whigs joined the nativist American or Know-Nothing party. In 1856, Millard Fillmore, the Know-Nothing candidate, carried Shreveport in his unsuccessful bid for the presidency. In 1860, the town threw its support to John Bell and the conservative Constitutional Union party. The larger rural vote in Caddo Parish, meanwhile, went overwhelmingly for the secessionist Democrat John Breckinridge.[11]

Unionist sentiment in Shreveport and elsewhere in Louisiana collapsed in face of increasing agitation for states' rights, particularly following Abraham Lincoln's election as president. On January 26, 1861, a state convention voted for secession. Following the surrender of Fort Sumter, men in Shreveport and elsewhere in Caddo Parish hurriedly prepared to leave for New Orleans to join the South's armed forces. Women bent over their sewing machines to make clothing and uniforms. But the uniforms of the Shreveport Grays were not completed when the company boarded the steamboat *Louis D'Or*. Women simply took up their sewing and boarded with them, continuing to work while en route. In the first year, Shreveport and other towns in the parish gave nineteen companies to the cause. Among other items going down the river to New Orleans were bells donated by the Methodist, Presbyterian, and Baptist churches to meet a shortage of metal for manufacturing cannons.[12]

During the Civil War, Shreveport saw its importance increase when it became a gateway for supplies arriving overland from Texas and Mexico. As a result, goods were generally more plentiful and could be purchased more cheaply locally than in other parts of the state.[13] Soldiers passed through from Arkansas, Texas, and other points west.

Refugees also came, mostly from parts of Louisiana occupied by the Union army, and these newcomers added to the growing wartime population of the town. Some brought slaves and household possessions and whatever else they could carry. To help these displaced people, and also to help soldiers and their families, local citizens organized various cultural events for their benefit, including plays, concerts, and tableaux. Among these efforts were two performances given by the "Confederate Minstrels" in December, 1862.

10. Joe Gray Taylor, "Slave Control in Louisiana," in Glenn R. Conrad (ed.), *Readings in Louisiana History* (New Orleans, 1978), 131, 137; Gute and Jeter, *Historical Profile*, 4.

11. Snyder, "Shreveport During the Civil War and Reconstruction," 43–44, 46; Peoples, "Politics, Parties, and Politicians," 146–47.

12. John D. Winters, *The Civil War in Louisiana* (Baton Rouge, 1963), 41, 76–77.

13. *Ibid.*, 54.

Another benefit performance—this one specifically for needy soldiers from Missouri—saw the glee club sing at the Gaiety Theatre in October, 1863. There was a second performance in December. Local ladies visited soldiers in the camps around the town to bring holiday cheer. In return, in February, 1864, the soldiers treated the ladies to a gala review and a mock battle, which were followed by a feast and short patriotic speeches.[14]

Before the war, Shreveport had enjoyed some light manufacturing. During the war it increased, as Confederate officials strove for self-sufficiency. Shops produced medicines, shoes, hats, and other supplies, and the Ordnance Bureau set up foundries, laboratories, and shops to manufacture ammunition. They could produce up to ten thousand rounds per day for small arms, and lesser amounts of shot and shell for artillery. Workmen also built the ironclad *Missouri,* which, unfortunately for the southern cause, surrendered in 1865 without having fired a shot. Meanwhile, townspeople worked to strengthen military defenses. By late 1863, there were no fewer than eighteen batteries and four forts protecting the town.[15]

In 1863, a fugitive Louisiana legislature held the first of three wartime sessions in the courthouse at Shreveport. Early the next year, General Edmund Kirby-Smith transferred the headquarters for the Trans-Mississippi Department to the town. With its strategic importance enhanced, Shreveport grew even busier, though its lack of a railroad was an inconvenience. The closest line ended at a point near the Texas border, and travelers had to complete the remaining few miles of the journey to Shreveport by stage. The Southern Pacific railway, later known as the Texas and Pacific, did not establish service to Shreveport until 1866.[16]

On January 26, 1864, Henry Watkins Allen became governor. Perhaps the finest administrator that the Confederacy produced, Allen immediately turned his attention to increasing preparedness for invasion in the part of the state that remained in Confederate hands. His promotion of public assistance for needy citizens and soldiers relieved many of the war's victims. His efforts to stabilize the currency, to a large degree, put the state back on a sound financial basis. Also, Allen's respect for civil liberties reined in overly zealous Confederate agents. During his residence in Shreveport, the governor lived simply in a small three-bedroom house.[17]

In early 1864 an expedition under the command of Major General Nathaniel P. Banks and Rear Admiral David Porter tried unsuccessfully to capture Shreveport during the Red River campaign. Union strategy was to cut off Confederate trade with Mexico and to isolate Texas. On April 8, outnumbered Confederate forces under General Richard Taylor repulsed Banks's army at the battle of Mansfield and caused the Federals to retreat. Meanwhile, another Union force under General Frederick Steele, which was advancing south

14. *Ibid.,* 211, 388, 403.

15. *Ibid.,* 321; Snyder, "Shreveport During the Civil War and Reconstruction," 100–106, 110; William N. Still, "The Confederate Ironclad *Missouri,*" *Southern Studies,* IV (1965), 101–10.

16. Tom Ruffin, "Early Railroading in the Ark-La-Tex," *Shreveport Magazine,* XXV (February, 1970), 19, 42–45.

17. Amos E. Simpson and Vincent Cassidy, "The Wartime Administration of Governor Henry W. Allen," in Conrad (ed.), *Readings in Louisiana History,* 205–209.

from Arkansas toward Shreveport in coordination with Banks's army, also grew discouraged and quit after encountering Confederate resistance.

It is unfortunate that no photographs of Shreveport during the war years have surfaced. They could supplement the sketchy contemporary descriptions that exist. For example, one visitor during this period was Lieutenant Colonel Arthur J. Fremantle of the British Coldstream Guards, who described the town as "rather decent looking." Photographers were at work in the area, however. In 1865 "C. & N. Olsen" advertised in the *Caddo Gazette*, offering to provide cartes de visite, ambrotypes, and photographs from their shop on Texas Street.[18]

Following General Robert E. Lee's surrender at Appomattox on April 9, 1865, uncertainty swept the Department of the Trans-Mississippi. As the hopelessness of the Confederate position grew apparent over the next few weeks, soldiers began to desert. Worse, some broke into military stores. On May 21 soldiers and civilians alike robbed the government's depots, leaving Shreveport's streets littered with castoff goods and official papers. Finally, a troop of Missouri soldiers appeared and restored order. They rounded up what pilfered goods they could and stored them at the courthouse. Federal occupying forces began arriving on June 6 under command of General Francis J. Herron, whose first order was to clean up the city's streets. Local slaves scarcely had time to adjust to their new freedom, which they heard proclaimed on June 10, before they watched black Federal soldiers march into town to take up garrison duty.

Until the removal of Federal forces on January 29, 1876, black soldiers made up the bulk of the occupying force.[19]

Following passage of the Reconstruction Acts by Congress and the ratification of the Louisiana state constitution of 1868, black adult males in the old Confederacy won the franchise. Many prominent Confederate veterans, in turn, were disqualified as voters. In Shreveport and Caddo Parish, this meant that the majority of those eligible to vote were black. Nevertheless, white Democrats continued to dominate the town's government for a few years. On May 27, 1871, Moses H. Crowell, who had briefly commanded Federal soldiers in Shreveport, became the first Republican mayor. This occurred after the legislature changed the town's trustee form of government. Governor Henry Clay Warmoth appointed Crowell and four administrators to serve on a new city council until their successors could be elected in November, 1872. Only three Republicans followed Crowell in office, however, before Democrat Samuel J. Ward became mayor in November, 1874. In 1878, a Democratic legislature restored the trustee form of government.

During Radical Reconstruction, Caddo Parish sent two black delegates to the convention that drew up the constitution of 1868. They were Caesar C. Antoine and former Union Army Captain James H. Ingraham. Antoine was a barber who had moved to Shreveport from New Orleans. Later, he won election to the state Senate, where he sponsored the bill that changed Shreveport's form of government. In 1872, Antoine was elected lieutenant governor to

18. *Shreveport Centennial*, 20; *Caddo Gazette*, September 15, 1865.

19. Winters, *The Civil War in Louisiana*, 424–27; Snyder, "Shreveport During the Civil War and Reconstruction," 146–50, 232.

serve under Governor William Pitt Kellogg. Other black legislators from Caddo Parish during Reconstruction included Moses Sterrett, William Harper, and the Reverend John Boyd. The black members of the delegation showed particular interest in securing state assistance for the public hospital in Shreveport that had been established in 1866 to care for indigent patients.[20]

Violent reaction to Radical Reconstruction occurred in Louisiana in 1868, as masked organizations such as the Knights of the White Camellia spread terror among blacks and Republican sympathizers. In North Louisiana, where violence appeared to be the worst, night riders whipped and murdered with impunity in the countryside. Planters threatened to discharge any tenants who voted for Republicans. In Caddo Parish, a single black man dared to vote Republican, and he paid with his life. Following the disputed election of 1872, many prominent men in Caddo Parish who were angry over the persistence of Reconstruction joined the White League, a paramilitary organization that sought to intimidate Republicans into abandoning office. In 1874 an incident at Coushatta in which five white Republicans were lynched created a national scandal, and wholesale arrests of White League members followed in parishes along the Red River. Among the most vehement defenders of the White League's actions was Henry J. Hearsey, editor of the Shreveport *Times*. One historian has described him as "a man of many hates," a "Dixie Don Quixote" of the Lost Cause.[21]

In response to the violence, a black man from Caddo Parish named Henry Adams, who was an ex-slave and a Union veteran, organized a committee in Shreveport to investigate injustices, especially terrorism, inflicted on freedmen. As a remedy, he proposed that the federal government set aside territory where blacks might migrate. Failing that, he asked for money to send blacks to Liberia. Following a meeting in Shreveport of some five thousand freedmen, Adams and the "Colonization Council," which had grown out of his committee's work, appealed unsuccessfully to President Hayes for help. By 1877, as Adams later testified before a select committee of the Senate in Washington, he had lost "all hope in the world" that conditions would improve for freedmen in the South. A compromise worked out on the national level had ended Reconstruction and restored the old ruling classes in Louisiana. Adams continued to work for various emigration groups, helping to inspire the great Exodus of 1879, a popular though essentially leaderless movement that put an estimated twenty thousand blacks from Louisiana, Mississippi, and Tennessee into motion for Kansas. Adams never went there himself. By then, he was con-

20. Charles Vincent, *Black Legislators in Louisiana During Reconstruction* (Baton Rouge, 1976), 129, 175–79; Snyder, "Shreveport During the Civil War and Reconstruction," 175–77, 185–87.

21. Allen W. Trelease, *White Terror: The Ku Klux Klan Conspiracy*

and Southern Reconstruction (New York, 1971), 130; Viola Carruth, *Caddo 1000: A History of the Shreveport Area from the Time of the Caddo Indians to the 1970s* (2nd ed., Shreveport, 1971), 77–83; William Ivy Hair, *Bourbonism and Agrarian Protest: Louisiana Politics, 1877–1900* (Baton Rouge, 1969), 24. Concerning this period, Snyder observes: "There is little proof that the Republican ascendancy in Shreveport was a time of inordinate corruption, much less inhumane oppression of Conservatives. Rather, it appears that the Democrats in Shreveport detested the local Radicals more for who they were and what they represented than what they did once in power." Snyder, "Shreveport During the Civil War and Reconstruction," 188.

vinced that Africa should be the ultimate destination of the migrants.[22]

In 1873 yellow fever inflicted the worst calamity that befell Shreveport during Reconstruction. The trouble reportedly began on August 19 when three men fell dead on Texas Street. As the number of deaths increased, Dr. W. T. D. Dalzell, an Episcopal priest and physician, vainly tried to alert the city's medical establishment to the danger of an epidemic. By September 1, evidence was clear, which created a panic among townspeople, many of whom jammed trains to leave. Dalzell stayed to help organize a local Howard Association to nurse the sick. A captain who landed his steamboat about this time recalled later that the livery stables were closed and the streetcars were not running. Blacks were considered to be immune, and many left the steamboats to serve as nurses to the fever's victims. Meanwhile, as word of the disaster spread, towns downriver refused to permit boats from Shreveport to land. At its peak, the epidemic killed 30 people a day. Twenty-two died in a single boardinghouse. Among the victims were 5 Catholic priests, 3 nuns, and the minister of the First Baptist Church. On November 15 the Shreveport *Times* listed the names of 759 victims of yellow fever. Mercifully, cool weather ended the epidemic.[23]

The yellow fever had broken out only a few days after a celebration that marked the opening of rail service between Shreveport and Dallas, which had been achieved by extension of the Texas and Pacific Railroad's line from Longview, Texas, west for 130 miles. Besides having a connection to Dallas, Shreveport also enjoyed rail service—via Marshall, Texas, and Texarkana—to Little Rock and St. Louis. By the end of 1882, the Texas and Pacific was also running trains from New Orleans to Shreveport and then on to Dallas and El Paso.[24]

Another significant improvement in local transportation occurred in 1873 when the Army Corps of Engineers, employing a crew under the command of Lieutenant E. A. Woodruff, cut a channel through the thirty miles of logjams that remained in the Red River above Shreveport. Thus, once Shreveport recovered its health from the great epidemic, it was assured of a more important position as an inland harbor. Unfortunately, yellow fever claimed Lieutenant Woodruff's life after he left his work on the river to help set up a hospital in town to nurse the sick. Accompanying the crew of the Corps of Engineers was a photographer named R. B. Talfor. Through his camera lens, we get a look at Shreveport's Commerce Street as it appeared in 1873 from the opposite bank of the Red River. The river flowed close to the strip of mostly small, two-story buildings—in fact, closer by several blocks than it flows today.[25]

22. Hair, *Bourbonism and Agrarian Protest*, 90–91; Eddie Vetter, "Henry Adams—Looking for a Way Out," Shreveport *Journal*, February 22, 1984. This article appeared in an award-winning supplement of the *Journal* on black history entitled "Freedom's Road." Several other contributions to this supplement are cited hereafter.

23. Tom Ruffin, "The Year of the Great Epidemic," *Shreveport*

Magazine, XXVIII (August, 1973), 34, 52; Henry C. Dethloff, "Paddlewheels and Pioneers on Red River, 1815–1915, and the Reminiscences of Captain M. L. Scovell," *Louisiana Studies*, VI (1967), 118–19.

24. Ruffin, "Early Railroading in the Ark-La-Tex," 46; Snyder, "Shreveport During the Civil War and Reconstruction," 204–206.

25. John Whitling Hall, "Geographical Views of Red River Valley,

Shreveport, like other southern cities and those in the nation as a whole, experienced rapid growth from 1880 until the Panic of 1893. A newspaper writer recalled the period fondly: "Electricity and pressed brick gave a new appearance to the city, and the people felt that they were 'out of the woods,' and having become masters of the advantages which had so long mastered them, were ready to move steadily along the lines of Nineteenth Century progress." By the mid-1890s, better-constructed buildings had replaced those of the city's infancy, and stores sported fronts with iron columns and cornices of stamped metal. Public buildings were heated with steam and lighted by gas and electricity. Grand homes appeared that reflected the transition in architectural styles from classical revival to Victorian. Even the police were said to be "handsomely upholstered." [26]

The surge in construction kept carpenters in steady work, and in 1887 they founded a union local in Shreveport. Fifteen years earlier, the typographers had organized what probably was the city's first trade union. With the appearance of other locals, there came into being an important labor movement, which by 1907 claimed twenty-one craft unions, represented collectively by the Central Trades and Labor Council. [27]

In Shreveport, as in other southern cities, realization

slowly came that certain public services were indispensable to a comfortable urban life. Eventually, this demand helped bring on a period of progressivism that, while still conservative in nature, speeded modernization. Nevertheless, to expand public services was difficult in the conservative post-Reconstruction years.

For one thing, the city had nearly defaulted on some bond issues a few years earlier and its finances remained uncertain; for another, the state constitution of 1879 limited local taxes to ten mills on the dollar. Besides, businessmen seemed to be more interested in spending public money to attract railroads. Thus, instead of undertaking a public project to build and operate the McNeil Street pumping station and its accompanying water and sewage systems, the city fathers awarded a franchise to a private individual. Operation began in 1887. Even then, the business community supported construction of the new systems more out of a desire for improved fire protection than for increased sanitation. [28]

Conditions that preceded construction of the water and sewage systems were abominable. Potable water was scarce and expensive, sanitation was inadequate, and fires threatened to exhaust available water supplies. People deemed water from the muddy Red River to be unfit for consumption. Those who could afford it bought their drinking water

1873," *North Louisiana Historical Association Journal*, XIII (Fall, 1982), 107–12.

26. Shreveport *Times*, "Illustrated Edition," 1894, pp. 1, 7.

27. Hubert Humphreys, "A History of the Shreveport Carpenters: Local 746," *North Louisiana Historical Association Journal*, XV (Winter, 1984), 1–2.

28. Terry S. Reynolds, "Cisterns and Fires: Shreveport, Louisiana, as a Case Study of the Emergence of Public Water Supply Systems in the South," *Louisiana History*, XXII (1981), 353–56, 366–67. Dependence upon a franchise to deliver this vital service proved unsatisfactory. After years of frustrations caused by poor service and dealing with private owners, the city assumed ownership in 1917.

from nearby springs for a nickle a bucket or fifty cents a barrel. Cisterns collected rainwater for washing and bathing and sometimes for drinking and cooking. Some poor people depended upon shallow wells, which often were contaminated by nearby privies. Streets were unpaved and at times littered with filth. Vacant lots were dumping grounds for household refuse and human excrement. After each epidemic, editors and other citizens railed against unsanitary practices, but apathy soon restored the filthy conditions. An early ordinance that required that privies be cleaned regularly probably was not enforced faithfully. The city did provide honey wagons to collect wastes from tubs under the privies. The wagons hauled their malodorous loads to the river for dumping. Even this elementary sanitation was ignored in poor neighborhoods.

Fire was a more constant threat to business interests in nineteenth-century Shreveport than was disease. A single blaze in 1854 destroyed almost a dozen businesses. On other occasions, inadequate supplies of water severely hampered efforts of voluntary fire companies. A system of six underground cisterns, holding from thirty thousand to fifty thousand gallons of water each, was built between 1867 and 1885, but it provided only limited protection. The cisterns leaked, forcing expensive maintenance repairs, and during dry weather the water level inside them fell dangerously low.[29]

Gradually, fire and sanitation problems were brought

under control. Following completion of the waterworks and sewage system, the city created a professional fire department in 1891, counting fifteen men on call in addition to the six regular firemen. By the decade's end, this force had grown to seventeen paid regulars, six mules, and two horses. In 1903 the city council passed an ordinance to require businesses such as restaurants and livery stables to use the city's sewer system for disposing of wastes instead of dumping them into the gutters. Two years later, city street crews joined a massive cleanup to eliminate breeding places for mosquitoes. The Board of Health fumigated all houses.[30]

Public transportation advanced in 1890 when the Shreveport Railway and Land Improvement Company introduced an electric streetcar system. The streetcars ran along a belt that was five and a quarter miles long. In 1902 this line was consolidated with that of a competing company that in the meantime had switched its cars over from mule power to electricity. In this era, expansion of streetcar services typically stretched the natural boundaries of a city, which till then had been defined as the distance a man could walk in about an hour. Along new routes, neighborhoods sprang up. In Highland Park, one of the first developments south of the old town, a streetcar line ran down White Street. Property owners petitioned the city commission in 1914 to change their street's name to Highland, both to avoid confusion for streetcar passengers and to give the street a more eupho-

29. *Ibid.,* 338–41, 344–45, 346–49. For a more exhaustive study of this subject, see Terry S. Reynolds, *A Cardinal Necessity: The McNeil Street Pumping Station and the Evolution of the Water Supply System of Shreveport, Louisiana,* National Architectural and Engineering Record,

Heritage Conservation and Recreation Service, Department of the Interior (Washington, D.C., 1980).

30. Shreveport *Times,* (centennial edition), June 28, 1935; David Buice, "Shreveport During the Progressive Era: An Overview," *North Louisiana Historical Association Journal,* XV (Fall, 1984), 152.

nious name.[31] Expansion of streetcar lines helped to disperse the population, thereby creating demand for new housing. Annexation of outlying areas often followed.

Another improvement for Shreveport was paved streets. In the late 1890s, work crews laid bricks to eliminate the problem of mud and dust that often made travel on the city's streets unpleasant. Mayor R. N. "Rube" McKellar devised an innovative way of financing this project. Many persons found guilty before him in mayor's court were ordered to pay a fine of $7.50 or 1,000 bricks. Those too poor to pay were sent to join the paving crews. Gradually, bond issues and the practice of paving through petition from abutting property owners replaced this expediency.[32]

Following the end of Reconstruction in Louisiana, public schools had suffered because of their association with Radical Republicanism. Many whites considered them to be places for poor children. Consequently, local governments were forbidden by law to levy taxes to pay for public education. In 1895 the Caddo Parish school board even had to sue the city of Shreveport to force officials to spend money on schools that had been collected in voluntary taxes for that purpose. Three years earlier, the Caddo board had opened the city's first public high school—available to whites only. Until then, private academies and seminaries provided what advanced schooling existed in Shreveport. The board had hired C. E. Byrd, a Virginian by birth, to come over from Monroe, Louisiana, as principal of the new high school. His first classrooms were in the old YMCA Building at the corner of Milam and Edwards streets, and to them he had attracted 40 students. Two more moves were required before the faculty and student body occupied a new school building at Hope and Texas streets, whose cornerstone was laid in 1898. Caddo Parish had eighty-nine public schools in 1894, but for that number it employed only 102 teachers. School sessions were nine months for the white schools and five months for the black ones. Ostensibly, this permitted black children to join their parents in the fields during the cultivating and harvesting seasons. School finances began to improve dramatically with ratification of the state constitution of 1898. It permitted both state and local taxation, along with the issuance of bonds, to support public schools. Within less than a decade, Shreveport had three more new schools. Meanwhile, enrollment in Caddo Parish increased steadily. In 1900, there were 2,539 white students and 3,612 black; by 1916 the numbers were 7,424 white and 7,332 black.[33]

During the Gilded Age, railroads replaced steamboats as the key to regional power. Shreveport's leaders offered substantial enticements to secure rail lines. To the Kansas City Southern railroad alone, the city and parish in 1895 agreed to pay a bonus of $325,000, with the last installment due in 1904. Sometimes the price was too high, however, as in 1887, when Shreveport leaders thought they might persuade Jay Gould to build a railroad in the area. He wanted a $50,000 subsidy, free depot grounds, and a free right-of-

31. Louis C. Hennick and E. Harper Charlton, *Street Railways of Louisiana* (Gretna, La., 1979), 59–64; Shreveport *Times,* February 18, 1914.
32. Buice, "Shreveport During the Progressive Era," 154.

33. *Ibid.,* 153–54; Shreveport *Times,* "Illustrated Edition," 1894, pp. 10, 21; Shreveport *Times* (centennial edition), June 28, 1935.

way through the city—all of this for a small branch line. In 1882, the Texas and Pacific reached farther westward, linking up with the Southern Pacific to provide Shreveport with service to the West Coast. When the T & P completed its line between Shreveport and New Orleans later that year, its trains had a through route from the Crescent City to the Pacific Ocean. In 1884 the Vicksburg, Shreveport and Pacific arrived from the east by building Shreveport's first bridge across the Red River. Two more lines that entered the city during the 1880s were the Houston and Shreveport, which provided direct service to Houston, and the St. Louis and Southwestern, which offered a new route to Memphis and St. Louis.[34]

River traffic reached its peak in 1883–1884, when twenty steamers ran regularly from Shreveport to New Orleans. During that fiscal year, they carried 108,000 bales of cotton, 270,000 pounds of hides and 35,000,000 board feet of lumber. For two months of the year in 1886, boats could travel as far upriver as Kiamatia, Texas, at the mouth of Kiamichi River. The boats traveling on the Red during this period ranged in size from one hundred to eight hundred tons. Competition from railroads reduced river traffic dramatically, however, so that by 1894, when the river was open to navigation year-round, only seven steamers operated between Shreveport and New Orleans.[35]

One could still acquire public lands in Caddo Parish for homesteading. In 1894, a total of 29,640 acres of federal lands remained unclaimed. Also, railroads had thousands of acres for sale from their own federal grants. Land in the hill country went for two to five dollars an acre. Good bottom land might go for as high as fifty dollars.[36] One difficulty was that prices for cotton were low, as fertile new lands in Texas contributed to overproduction.

Promoters attempted to persuade cotton farmers to diversify. An exhibit at the Louisiana State Fair and Shreveport Exhibition of 1891 demonstrated various other crops that land in the area might produce. Among them were millet, hemp, wheat, and sweet and Irish potatoes. Such efforts were limited in part because of the crop lien system, which permitted farmers to borrow against their next crop. Under this system, lenders usually preferred that cotton be grown. They knew it could be easily sold, even at low prices. In fact, the fair itself went out of business in 1894 when the price for cotton fell to four and a half cents a pound. In 1906 promoters organized a new state fair, which continues today.[37]

Hard times in agriculture did not produce much sympathy in Shreveport for the political and economic reforms demanded by American farmers in the 1880s and 1890s. Nevertheless, on October 12, 1887, the National Farmers' Alliance and Co-operative Union of America held its first national meeting in the city. The organization, created when the Texas Farmers' Alliance joined forces with the Louisiana Farmers' Union, championed the interests of beleaguered hill-country farmers. It proposed an elaborate plan

34. *Shreveport of To-Day* (Shreveport, 1904), 24; Hair, *Bourbonism and Agrarian Protest,* 111–12; Ruffin, "Early Railroading in the Ark-La-Tex," 46–47.

35. Carl Newton Tyson, *The Red River in Southwestern History* (Norman, 1981), 154–56.

36. Shreveport *Times,* "Illustrated Edition," 1894, pp. 8, 10.

37. *Ibid.,* 10; Shreveport *Times* (centennial edition), June 28, 1935.

for restructuring the nation's monetary system to make credit easier for farmers to obtain and to reduce the influence of eastern banks. The Alliance also demanded that government regulate—or even own—railroads and telegraph companies. For the next three years, the Alliance burst across the cotton South and into the Great Plains, drawing as many as three million people to its cause, including many from the parishes of North Louisiana. The emotionalism that flowed from this movement helped lay the basis for the founding in 1892 of the Populist party, whose radical platform included free silver, an income tax, and reclamation of railroad lands.[38]

In Louisiana's Fourth District, the Populist party sought unsuccessfully in 1892 to defeat the conservative congressman from Shreveport, Newton C. Blanchard, who had held his office since 1881. Toward Blanchard's opponent, Thomas J. Guice, the Democrats hurled such epithets as "Greasy Guice" and "the great unwashed from the forks of the crick."[39] In this election and in the governor's race four years later, the city gave little support to Populism. The outbreak of protest threatened conservatives' paternalistic rule. It also raised the specter of black voters joining the Populists' cause in numbers sufficient to win elections. Populists across the South emphasized common problems that farmers of both races shared, and blacks formed their own alliance as a counterpart to the white organization. This brief attempt to overcome white prejudice and to promote class

solidarity failed, however, and by 1896 Populism was largely spent.

In Louisiana's bitter gubernatorial election of that year, some conservatives openly advocated fraud as a means of defeating John N. Pharr, who ran as the fusion candidate of both Populists and Republicans. The Shreveport *Evening Judge* declared: "It is the religious duty of Democrats to rob Populists and Republicans of their votes whenever and wherever the opportunity presents itself and any failure to do so will be a violation of true Louisiana Democratic teaching. The Populists and Republicans are our legitimate political prey. Rob them! You bet! What are we here for?" Pharr lost in Shreveport by 3,210 to 227. Two years later, the Democratic oligarchy succeeded in disfranchising most of the state's blacks, along with many poor whites. The main instrument for this purpose was the new constitution of 1898, which introduced an ingenious device known as the "grandfather clause." This mechanism exempted from literacy and property tests any male who had been entitled to vote in 1867, along with his sons and grandsons. In face of restrictive registration laws, the number of registered black voters fell from 130,344 in 1897 to just 1,342 in 1904. White registration fell from 164,088 to 91,716 in that same period.[40] Gradually, disaffected whites returned to the Democratic party. Another generation would pass before the spirit of Populism revived, this time in the politics of Huey P. Long.

As life on the farms worsened, many men sought employ-

38. Hair, *Bourbonism and Agrarian Protest,* 149–53; Tom Ruffin, "Agrarian Crusade," *Shreveport Magazine,* XXXII (October, 1977), 22, 24.

39. Hair, *Bourbonism and Agrarian Protest,* 206, 230–32.

40. *Ibid.,* 260, 263; C. Vann Woodward, *Origins of the New South, 1877–1913* (Baton Rouge, 1951), 334, 342–43.

ment in the forests and in the lumber mills. Demand for lumber came in part from construction of railroads, which picked up dramatically in the 1880s and continued into the twentieth century. Some of the mills grew into towns that were populated by their work forces and served by their private railroad lines. One such community was Allentown, which the firm of Allen Brothers and Wadley established on several thousand acres of land north of Haughton, Louisiana, in 1891. A contemporary description plays down the dreary aspects of such towns: "There are no drones or idlers at Allentown, and none are allowed to remain there—all must work or move on. From 120 to 140 men are kept constantly employed. The employees live within a short distance of the mill in houses which were built for their comfort and convenience by the company. . . . In a word, it is a model town. It has its own school house, church and Sunday school, a resident physician, a large store which is stocked from one end to the other with general merchandise, and many other comforts."[41]

In 1894 a writer for a Shreveport newspaper complained about a "harmful reputation that in some unaccountable manner attached itself to the inhabitants of this city for inertness and inactivity." In reality, the work ethic was strong in Northwest Louisiana. For ten and twelve hours a day, six days a week, workers kept to their jobs, ever fearful that hard times might strip away their livelihoods. Competition for work put pressure on race relations in southern cities, as whites demanded—and usually received—the best jobs. In the twentieth century, for example, whites increasingly pushed blacks from skilled occupations, such as barbering and carpentry, that had allowed the latter to serve white customers and employers. A union local in Shreveport voted down a motion in 1901 to organize black carpenters, who for the most part were drawing common laborers' wages. In 1921 the white carpenters' local took action against builders who employed black carpenters, though it made exceptions for cases where houses were being built in black neighborhoods.[42]

Beginning in the 1870s, landlords found the shotgun house to be the most practical type of housing for Shreveport's growing work force. A number of these long, usually two- or three-room houses could be placed onto a single lot. Blacks who migrated to southern cities after the Civil War often were pushed onto land along railroad tracks, in low-lying areas, and in other undesirable locations. White families, however, also lived in some of these areas, such as St. Paul's Bottoms, located west of the downtown. There blacks generally inhabited the low sections, while whites had their houses on the higher ground. In the backyards of many houses in middle-class white neighborhoods—or perhaps in alleys nearby—were small structures where black servants lived.[43]

By the mid-1890s, Shreveport's population was close to

41. Shreveport *Times,* "Illustrated Edition," 1894, p. 16.

42. *Ibid.,* 13; Blaine A. Brownell, "The Urban South Comes of Age," in Blaine A. Brownell and David R. Goldfield (eds.), *The City in Southern History* (Port Washington, N.Y., 1977), 139; Humphreys, "A History of the Shreveport Carpenters," 9.

43. Donnis Arnold (ed.), *St. Paul's Bottoms to Ledbetter Heights: A Succession of Changing Attitudes* (Shreveport, 1985); Brownell, "The Urban South Comes of Age," 138.

sixteen thousand. Among the city's amenities—along with the waterworks and sewage system, professional fire and police departments, and electric streetcars—were telephones, electric lights, and a public high school. By this time many of the important commercial establishments and offices were considerably removed from the older areas along the riverfront. Handsome public buildings, heated with steam and lighted by gas and electricity, gave the city a more mature appearance. On the corner of Texas and Marshall streets stood the imposing federal post office and customhouse. Across from it was the parish courthouse, built of red brick and limestone in the popular Romanesque revival style. Just down the street was the Grand Opera House. At the head of Texas sat First Methodist Church, a Gothic structure, and not far away rose the steeple of First Baptist Church at Texas and McNeil. Brick crosswalks laid in the rock and gravel permitted pedestrians to step conveniently across the street, though one still had to be careful to avoid manure left by horses. Quick transportation to other parts, including the newer subdivisions, could be had by boarding one of the open-sided electric streetcars that traveled Texas Street regularly.[44]

A ride on a streetcar was a good way to cool off on summer evenings, though a visitor might prefer to walk and inspect some of the grand residences that ringed the commercial district, such as the Victorian mansion of Newton C. Blanchard at Common and Cotton streets. If one was not lucky enough to be a guest in such a home, there was the Phoenix Hotel at Texas and Market, renowned for its modern rooms and reasonable prices. Also nearby was the Serwich Hotel, where one might satisfy his hunger by pulling up a high stool at Frank Serwich's lunch counter. Tables were available in the Ladies' Dining Room Parlor. The hotel also maintained a bar for gentlemen to enjoy their beer and whiskey.[45]

Besides frequenting the Grand Opera House during the performing season, people enjoyed amateur theatrics and attended informal concerts given by such groups as the Shreveport Mandolin Club. In 1896, Charles Rettig, who had come to Shreveport to play the bass violin for the orchestra at the Grand, gathered around him some of the city's most talented male musicians to form the famous Rettig's Band. Among their number was N. S. Allen, an architect who designed many of the city's grand houses and buildings. Also in the group was Joe Dambly, a photographer whose studio on Milam Street produced many of the portraits that have survived from the era.[46]

Horse racing and the gambling that accompanied it helped to draw crowds to state fairs, and typically there were three to five races per session. In the early years, this form of entertainment drew little opposition from the clergy. Shreveport also had a private racetrack called Caddo Downs, where the city's present fairgrounds are located. The sport was the most popular in America until the rise of professional baseball. As historian Gunther Barth wrote: "Horse

44. Shreveport *Times,* "Illustrated Edition," 1894, pp. 7, 8. For descriptions of old buildings that are still standing, see Bailey Thomson (ed.), *Historic Shreveport: A Guide* (Shreveport, 1980).

45. Shreveport *Times,* "Illustrated Edition," 1894, pp. 4, 13; Shreveport *Journal* (centennial edition), June 27, 1935.

46. J. Ed Howe, "Rettig's Band," *Shreveport Magazine,* II (November, 1947), 32.

racing fascinated city people. They craved rural scenes, and the racetrack recaptured some of the gaiety and turmoil of a horse fair in the country." [47] People in cities were accustomed to being around horses. The animals pulled their carriages, hauled heavy loads, carried firemen to burning houses, and served as handsome mounts for gentlemen and even for some ladies who had sidesaddles.

There were baseball teams in the city at least by 1885, when the O.K. Baseball Club declared itself state champion outside of New Orleans. Shreveport had a semipro team by 1892, managed by Pete Weckbecker. Some of its members went on to play for important professional teams in the North. Beginning in 1895, Shreveport fielded its own professional teams in various leagues, including the Southern Association and the Texas League. By 1904, the city's ballpark could seat more than two thousand fans, who sweltered in the bleachers in the summertime. [48]

Toward the end of the century, particularly as paving of the major streets progressed, bicycles became popular. Skirts were shortened across the nation by two inches to permit female participation in the sport. Lead weights in the hems held the skirts respectably in place. Some riders in Shreveport could not resist the sidewalks, which caused the city fathers to pass an ordinance to prohibit the practice. A writer in the Shreveport *Times* warned those who might violate the law: "A police officer might see them when they least think about it. Don't try it too often, young gentlemen." [49]

Advertisements for liquor appeared frequently in the newspapers. Shreveport may have deserved its reputation as a "city of churches," but there was a big thirst to be quenched during the week. Alcohol was sold openly until 1908, when voters made Caddo Parish dry. The proposition carried by only sixty-two votes, with rural voters making up the bulk of those in favor. Private possession of alcohol was permissible, however, and this encouraged a number of ingenious subterfuges. There also grew up illegal drinking establishments, especially in St. Paul's Bottoms, where prostitution already flourished under an official arrangement that permitted brothels to operate so long as they remained within the designated "segregated district." [50]

Before prohibition, the city had several breweries, which provided a variety of local labels, including Shreveport Select and Caddo. Caddo Brewery, whose president was Adolphus Busch of the Anheuser-Busch Brewery of St. Louis, produced enough electricity to freeze 250 tons of ice every day. Its rival, the Shreveport Brewery, employed fifty people and produced forty thousand barrels of beer a year, including one brand called Malt Extract, which it promoted as a particularly nourishing "nerve food." One booster went so far as to declare, "The time is near when Shreveport will occupy the same relative position in the beer industry of the South that Milwaukee holds in the North." Advertisements suggested that these fermented beverages were good for

47. Garnie W. McGinty, "Horse Racing in North Louisiana, 1911–1914," *North Louisiana Historical Association Journal* IV (Fall, 1971), 25–27; Gunther Barth, *City People: The Rise of Modern City Culture in Nineteenth-Century America* (New York, 1980), 155.

48. Carruth, *Caddo 1000,* p. 110; Shreveport *Journal* (centennial edition), June 27, 1935; *Shreveport of To-Day,* 31.

49. Shreveport *Times,* July 1, 1897.

50. Goodloe Stuck, *Annie McCune: Shreveport Madam* (Baton Rouge, 1981), 76–78.

everyone, including children. Thus, one might read, "Schlitz's bottle beer to please the ladies, and fatten the babies."[51]

Local boosters persistently desired to increase the population and the number of industries. "Immigration is needed first and foremost," declared one observer in 1894. "Our population is not dense enough to utilize our wonderful advantages." If only prospective settlers and capitalists from the North and East would take a look at Northwest Louisiana, local promoters thought, then they would see the "glorious possibilities to be accomplished in addition to the already established enormous facilities for handling every manner of freight, both by river and rail." The law provided that, should a capitalist locate a new factory in the city, his property would be exempt from state and municipal taxes for ten years.[52]

During the first decade of the twentieth century, southern cities underwent their greatest rates of growth, as the region gradually moved from an agricultural to an industrial economy. For Shreveport, the discovery of oil in the northern part of Caddo Parish in 1905 provided an additional impetus. From 1900 to 1910, the city's population grew from 16,013 to 28,015, a 75 percent increase. City fathers organized to preach what might be called "the gospel of Shreveport." A group named the Progressive League promoted immigration, which it declared to be among the chief concerns of a "wide awake citizenship." In 1904 the league published an illustrated booklet to advertise the area's virtues. By then, the city claimed more than six miles of paved streets

and alleys, eleven miles of sanitary sewers, seventeen miles of water mains, nine miles of electric streetcar rails, two telephone systems, and a hundred streetlights. All of this represented progress, in the opinion of the city's businessmen.[53]

In 1910 the newly organized chamber of commerce bragged that SHREVEPORT SPELLS SUCCESS. Emphasis remained on attracting newcomers through extensive advertising of the area's virtues. There was more immediate work to do as well, for Shreveport felt the bad effects of discriminatory rail rates that gave an advantage to cities in Texas and Arkansas. The chamber entered the legal fight against this practice.[54]

In the countryside, meanwhile, the boll weevil had brought a new misery to farmers by 1905, many of whom tried to scratch out a quarter of a bale to the acre on thin hill-country soils. To return to the theme of diversification and perhaps catch the eye of some well-to-do outsider looking to buy farmland, a group of businessmen, planters, and bankers organized the new state fair in 1906. Among the ideas they promoted was the raising of livestock, particularly dairy cattle. The traditional southern way was to turn animals loose in the woods and on marginal land, where they might forage for themselves. Advocates of modern herding held out a prospect of converting cotton lands into pastures. Eventually, the idea caught on, but not until devotion to cotton had driven more generations of farmers to de-

51. *Shreveport of To-Day,* 48, 56; Shreveport *Times,* October 5, 1890.
52. Shreveport *Times,* "Illustrated Edition," 1894, pp. 7, 13.

53. Brownell, "The Urban South Comes of Age," 123–24; U.S. Bureau of the Census, *1980 Census of Population: Number of Inhabitants,* I, 177; *Shreveport of To-Day,* esp. 7.
54. Shreveport *Times* (centennial edition), June 28, 1935.

spair. At the new fair, people also saw their first automobile race. In 1906 drivers reached speeds of twenty-five miles an hour, presaging a time when ordinary people might drive at such velocities themselves.[55]

In 1904 a tiny engine company at 220 Crockett advertised itself as the agent for Oldsmobile automobiles. The shop could hardly match the impressive livery stable of A. M. McWilliams on Market Street. Within a few years, however, livery stables were obsolete, and demand for automobiles created a new support industry of dealerships, garages, and service stations. In Cedar Grove, an incorporated industrial community just outside of Shreveport, there was even an assembly plant, where from 1918 to 1922 workers put together Bour-Davis automobiles.[56] As ownership of automobiles became more common, people depended less upon streetcars, a trend that encouraged even greater dispersal of the population.

Another development in transportation was important for Shreveport and its hinterland. In 1912 the federal Interstate Commerce Commission, acting on a complaint from the Louisiana Railroad Commission, ordered railroads to cease discrimination in their rates against Shreveport and in favor of Texas cities that traded in the same markets. Texas railroad carriers charged intrastate rates on traffic from Dallas and other Texas cities to points in eastern Texas that were considerably cheaper than the interstate rates that the ICC had established for traffic from Shreveport into eastern Texas. For example, the freight on a wagon shipped from

Shreveport to Marshall, Texas, a distance of 42 miles, was 56 cents per hundredweight. Shipping that same wagon from Dallas to Marshall, a distance of 147.7 miles, would cost only 36.8 cents per hundredweight. The ICC ordered that intrastate rates in Texas be equalized with interstate rates. When the United States Supreme Court received the "Shreveport Case" on appeal, it rendered a landmark decision that upheld the ICC's action in reshaping the railroad rate structure. The court held that Congress through the ICC had authority to ensure that a state did not impede the flow of interstate commerce.[57]

Thus, less than a century after the federal government had paid Captain Shreve to clear the great logjams from the Red River, a federal agency removed a modern obstacle to local commerce—unfair and onerous railroad-rate discrimination. Once more, Washington's long reach proved beneficial to Shreveport.

57. *Houston E. and W. Texas Railway Co.* v. *U.S.,* U.S. Supreme Court, 1914 (234 U.S. 342); Tom Ruffin, "Fight for Economic Survival," *Shreveport Magazine,* XXXII (November, 1977), esp. 26; James P. Baughman, "The Evolution of Rail-Water Systems of Transportation in the Gulf Southwest, 1836–1890," *Journal of Southern History,* XXXIV (1968), 357.

55. *Ibid.*
56. *Shreveport of To-Day,* 55, 71; Carruth, *Caddo 1000,* p. 135.

Photograph by R. B. Talfor. U.S. Army Corps of Engineers Collection, LSUS Archives.

Lieutenant E. A. Woodruff of the United States Army Corps of Engineers and his crew brought along R. B. Talfor in 1873 to photograph the removal of a thirty-mile stretch of logjams in the Red River above Shreveport. This obstacle to commerce on the upper Red was left over from the "Great Raft," which Captain Henry Miller Shreve had begun clearing in 1833. Shreve had actu-ally succeeded in removing the shifting logjams, only to see part of the Raft re-form by 1839 and again block the river's channel. So thick were the logs and rotting debris that at some places on the river and its tributaries one could walk from bank to bank, as the man in this photograph appears to be doing.

26

The steamer *Aid* (LEFT) was the flagship of the small fleet of boats that Woodruff used to attack the logjams. Built in Pittsburgh in 1869, the twin-hull vessel was 136 feet long and was propelled by two steam engines. George S. Woodruff, brother of the lieutenant, recalled that the *Aid* originally was a wrecking boat, designed to raise sunken steamboats on the Mississippi and Ohio rivers. Lieutenant Woodruff found the *Aid* in St. Louis and bought it for twenty thousand dollars. He took the boat to New Orleans, where workmen refitted it with cranes, windlasses, and other devices useful for tackling some of the enormous logs that formed a logjam's heart. On the bow they placed a steam-driven saw. The *Aid* left New Orleans around the end of November, 1872, pushing two smaller snagboats ahead of it. The group did not arrive at the logjams until the end of January because of delays caused by low water.

RIGHT: The crew aboard the *Aid* hauls in a log to be cut up.

Photograph by R. B. Talfor. U.S. Army Corps of Engineers Collection, LSUS Archives.

28

Photograph by R. B. Talfor. U.S. Army Corps of Engineers Collection, LSUS Archives.

Photograph by R. B. Talfor. U.S. Army Corps of Engineers Collection, LSUS Archives.

During the late winter and early spring of 1873, Woodruff's crew worked to clear the logjams, sometimes employing a steam saw mounted on a flatboat (LEFT). Besides accumulations of logs and debris, from which trees and other vegetation grew, there were also sandbars and deposits of silt. Blasts from nitroglycerin occasionally interrupted the monotonous sawing, hacking, and pulling at the embedded logs. The photographer Talfor, meanwhile, roamed the banks with his tripod-mounted eight-by-ten camera. Like photographers of the Civil War, who had also tried to catch the action of great events, Talfor had to haul a field darkroom with him, so that he could paint his emulsions on glass plates. He exposed these while they were still wet in the camera.

On May 16 Woodruff's crew opened a channel through a part of the Raft wide enough for the *R. T. Bryarly* (ABOVE), loaded with freight bound for the upper regions of the Red, to pass through. On another boat, dignitaries from Shreveport cheered this victory. Commerce could now move freely up and down the river, though within a generation trains would replace most of the big boats.

Both Lieutenant Woodruff and the *Bryarly* suffered tragedies soon after their triumphs. The officer died in an epidemic of yellow fever that swept away 759 victims in Shreveport in the fall of 1873. (George Woodruff succeeded his brother in command of the project and remained on duty until April, 1874.) The 150-foot *Bryarly* sank three years later, after hitting an obstruction in the Red River.

ABOVE: The Red River ran closer to Shreveport's Commerce Street in 1873 than it does today. Boats could tie up within a short distance of the stores. Along this strip grew up the first downtown.

LEFT: A visitor to the city in the late 1870s might have encountered muddy streets and oxen-drawn wagons along Texas Street. In the distance is a streetcar drawn by mules. The Shreveport City Railroad Company laid tracks for the first streetcar line in 1870. It ran along Texas Street, Common Street, and Texas Avenue to the municipal limits. The streetcar was slow, and passengers sometimes had to disembark in the mud when the vehicle ran off the tracks.

Although not taken until 1903, this photograph provides a sense of
how Commerce Street appeared in the early years.

33

Until snapshot cameras appeared around 1888, photography was too complicated for anyone but serious practitioners, many of whom made their living at the craft. Their studios turned out portraits on order, often against elaborate backdrops lit by sunlight from a window. After 1879 gelatin plates, which could be developed long after exposure, replaced the awkward wet plates, thereby freeing the photographer from his portable darkroom.

LEFT: This curious photograph, probably taken in 1892, shows a photographer at work, though neither his name nor the names of his subjects are known. The natural backdrop is formed by the floodwaters of the Red River, which are flowing into the old bed of Silver Lake, just south of Shreveport.

ABOVE: The steamer *C. E. Satterlee,* owned by the Texas and Pacific Railroad, docks at Shreveport in about 1890. River traffic on the Red River gradually yielded to competition from rails.

Photograph by Shreveport Camera Club. Stockslager-Walters-Weaks Collection, LSUS Archives.

A member of the Shreveport Camera Club took this portrait of his friend by the old fishing hole on Sand Beach near Shreveport, *ca.* 1896.

The Country

The hinterland nourished the city's growth, providing the great cash crop cotton and natural riches of lumber and petroleum. The simpler life of fields and woods, old-time religion and fishing holes played powerfully on the imaginations of city folk, even as they bragged of their new electric lights, paved streets, and traveling musical shows.

RIGHT: Zachariah Taylor Brooks of Union Parish poses with his dogs Bob and Lee *ca.* 1900. A veteran of the Civil War, Brooks loved to hunt, though he suffered from muscular dystrophy.

Community Fair Collection, LSUS Archives. Donated by Fran Walker.

The custom of "dinner on the grounds" often turned church into a
social outing, as it did for this group in Coushatta in 1884.

Community Fair Collection, LSUS Archives. Donated by Ann Clanton.

Rural Free Delivery brought relief from the isolation and loneliness of the country. Through subscriptions to magazines and newspapers, people could follow the news, learn farming methods, and even cultivate their literary tastes. Will Huckaby and his horses (ABOVE) pause along their route, which took them from Ringgold to Castor and then to Social Springs in Bienville Parish. The photograph dates from about 1912.

Little Helena Hutchinson Hearne feeds poultry in the backyard of the "big house" on the Hutchinson family's plantation at Caspiana in Caddo Parish, *ca.* 1900. She is dressed more for the camera than for farm chores.

The family of Mitchell Joel Moore of Ringgold, *ca.* 1900.

Family outings provided entertainment as well as opportunities to seek cool places during the summertime. The Colvin and Mitchell families enjoy the shade near D'Arbonne Bayou, *ca.* 1904.

Respectable young women of the time might seek their education at a female academy, such as this one at Minden, *ca.* 1895. Note that the lady in black to the far left has her back turned to the camera.

42

Community Fair Collection, LSUS Archives. Donated by Mr. and Mrs. W. B. Watson.

Community Fair Collection, LSUS Archives. Donated by Mrs. Nelson Barnette.

Before consolidation of rural schools, teachers had students of all ages. Bossier Parish's Brushy High School (LEFT) in 1902 reflects the meager efforts during the era to educate rural youth.

Grand Cane High School (ABOVE) in De Soto Parish was larger, but rustic nonetheless. The year is about 1898. The man standing on the porch is believed to be Professor George Williamson.

Community Fair Collection, LSUS Archives. Donated by Ernest R. Roberson.

Community Fair Collection, LSUS Archives. Donated by Mrs. Joe A. Price.

In the 1880s, the pace of railroad construction set new records in the South, particularly in Texas. Northwest Louisiana's virgin forests helped to meet the demands for lumber by the railroads and other industries. Some large companies even constructed towns to house their crews and operations and built railroad tracks deep into the woods to haul out timber. Vast forested areas were thus laid bare.

LEFT: Workers for the Fred B. Dubach Lumber Company pause for a moment in their task of wrestling logs onto a rail car in Lincoln Parish for transportation to the mill in 1904.

ABOVE: A photographer found this group of loggers in Black Lake Swamp near Ringgold in Bienville Parish in 1908. The five logs came from the same tree.

LEFT: This small train hauled logs in Claiborne Parish, *ca.* 1910. The man on the left is Guss Nation, and standing next to him is Lawrence Cline. The black man is unidentified.

ABOVE: At home in a logging camp in Bernice, *ca.* 1905. Members of the family are Ben H. Butler, Sr., India Cameron Butler, and their two sons, Harris Dewey (holding the pig) and O. Louie Butler. The tent has a wooden floor.

Photograph by Price Studio. Tom Bell Collection, LSUS Archives.

Discovery of oil in Texas and Oklahoma around the turn of the century encouraged explorers to drill wells in Caddo Parish, where natural gas was known to exist. In 1905 a well called Savage No. 1 produced five barrels of oil, and interest increased in local prospects. Two years later a crew drilled 2,180 feet to tap the Caddo pool and bring in a well that pumped 190 barrels a day. By 1911, even Caddo Lake bristled with derricks. Technology in the Caddo field was crude and wasteful. Drillers burned off natural gas, there being no pipelines to transport this resource. Abandoned "wild gassers" became a common sight, and their flames lit up the evening skies. Huge craters grew where the gas escaped, and several derricks along with drilling machinery fell in. According to historian William I. Hair, "Each day by 1907, an estimated 70,000 cubic feet of Caddo's natural gas simply vanished into the atmosphere. . . . But for the next six years this squandering of Louisiana's most precious resource actually increased." He estimates that the amount wasted probably exceeded two hundred billion cubic feet.

Accidents also could produce spectacular fires, as when a spark set off Producers Oil Company's Harrell No. 7 well in 1911, soon after it came in. For thirty days, workers fought the blaze, shooting water and steam—and even cannonballs—at the inferno's mouth. Finally, someone thought of digging a tunnel two hundred feet to the well's casing and diverting the oil and gas away from the flame. It worked!

LEFT: Members of the crew pause at the tunnel's mouth, as smoke from the fire billows in the background. After the fire was extinguished, the well became a big producer.

Once the fever from new discoveries subsided, the oil business settled into routine chores. RIGHT: A pipeline crew takes time for "dinner" near Trees, Louisiana, in the Caddo Oil Field, *ca.* 1914.

Photograph by Price Studio, Community Fair Collection, LSUS Archives. Donated by Mrs. Julius Horton.

Photograph by Price Studio. Tom Bell Collection, LSUS Archives.

Vivian was among the small towns near Shreveport that grew up during the first oil boom. Discoveries attracted more than just wildcatters and roughnecks, as word of prosperity spread. Among those who came to entertain in 1912 was a daredevil named Eckhart, who inflated his hot-air balloon on the main street of Vivian (ABOVE).

RIGHT: Once aloft, Eckhart suspended himself upside down from the balloon, which was far overhead. His dangling body is barely visible in the middle of the photograph.

ECKHARTS PERFORMANCE ON LOUISIANA AVE.

Photograph by Price Studio. Tom Bell Collection, LSUS Archives.

Stockslager-Walters-Weaks Collection, LSUS Archives.

By the late 1800s, the refinement and opportunities of city life contrasted with the monotony of the country, though popular sentiment continued to extol the virtues of the latter. LEFT: There are contentment and satisfaction in the faces of these Shreveport residents on the porch of the Stringfellow home on Fairfield Avenue, *ca.* 1910. Thomas Levert Stringfellow, seated in the wicker chair, was a banker. Next to him on the right are his wife, Georgia Howell Stringfellow, and their two children. The man in the background and the woman with the hat are Mr. and Mrs. S. J. Harmon, daughter and son-in-law of the Stringfellows. The infant and the other woman probably are members of the Harmon family.

But city people still endured many of the discomforts that afflicted country folk. There was no assurance of pure drinking water until after 1900, and contagion frequently swept away the young and the weak. Summer heat sometimes made sleep impossible, and the hot air carried a mixture of dust and dried horse or mule manure from the unpaved streets. ABOVE: A ground-level view of Shreveport, *ca.* 1890, from the head of Texas Street, looking toward the river, reveals the high steeple of the First Baptist Church on the left. A little farther down the street is the tower of the old post office.

54

Steamers such as the *C. W. Howell* (ABOVE) regularly traveled the Red River when this photograph was taken about 1885, but the bridge in the background foreshadows the demise of river traffic. The Vicksburg, Shreveport and Pacific Railroad bridged the river in 1884, connecting Shreveport to points east. The bridge's center section could swing open to permit boats to pass.

RIGHT: The Vicksburg, Shreveport and Pacific bridge also carried horse-drawn traffic and pedestrians. This photograph dates from *ca.* 1905.

Community Fair Collection, LSUS Archives. Donated by First National Bank, Shreveport.

Photograph by T. M. Elliott. Shreveport Chamber of Commerce Collection, LSUS Archives.

Community Fair Collection, LSUS Archives. Donated by Stephen R. Smith.

The Shreveport Railway and Land Improvement Company introduced electric streetcars to the city on October 4, 1890. Tracks ran along a belt five and a quarter miles long. It took twenty-eight minutes to make the trip. For the inaugural run, politicians joined lawyers, journalists, educators, and other prominent citizens in the four brightly decked cars (LEFT). In the background is the Phoenix Hotel at Texas and Market streets. In 1893 the competing Shreveport City Railroad Company added electric cars.

Merger created the Shreveport Traction Company in 1902. It re-tained that name until 1914, when it became the Shreveport Railways Company. Extension of streetcar lines, and sometimes the creation of new transit companies, often accompanied real-estate developments.

ABOVE: The open sides of the streetcars, like this one pictured *ca.* 1905, invited passengers to take a ride around the "belt" on summer evenings.

58

Shreveport had some handsome, substantial buildings by the late 1890s. One was the post office and customhouse (LEFT), at Texas and Marshall streets. The building was completed in 1887, and the photograph reveals how it looked in 1900.

Construction of the Shreveport High School (RIGHT) on Hope Street in 1898 permitted Professor C. E. Byrd to move the senior-level classes to their first permanent home. A Virginian by birth, Byrd came to Shreveport in 1892 to establish a high school for white students. He called his first student body to order in the old YMCA building at Edwards and Milam. Students and teachers moved twice to temporary locations, including one floor of the junior high school. Finally, the school board of Caddo Parish committed itself to building a new high school.

The state constitution forbade special property taxes and bonds to support public schools, forcing local school boards to depend upon subscription drives to supplement insufficient revenues. The school board plunged ahead with its construction plans anyway. Luckily, a new constitution replaced the old document in 1898. It granted school boards broad taxing powers.

General Collection, LSUS Archives. Courtesy *River Cities* magazine.

60

LEFT: Demand for entertainment in Shreveport led to construction of the Grand Opera House in 1889 at Texas and Edwards streets. The theater could seat 1,200 customers, and it had a magnificent stage. The Grand opened with James O'Neal in the title role of *King Lear.* Thereafter, advertisements of attractions carried names of well-known entertainers, and performing companies often came over from Houston for one-night engagements. When Harry and Simon Ehrlich took over the management, following the death of Leon M. Carter, they began featuring the popular Al G. Fields Minstrels, who paraded through the downtown to advertise their show.

Around 1900, the best seats usually went for one dollar. Before performances, newsboys hawked their papers in front of the theater, where good customers were likely to appear. Among regular theatergoers was Annie McCune, Shreveport's best-known madam, from the red-light district in St. Paul's Bottoms. So large was her own bottom that she required an enlarged seat—one reserved for her.

The Grand's bill of professional entertainment lasted only four months out of the year. In the remaining months, amateur groups often staged productions. Vaudeville appeared by 1908. Admission to those shows was ten and fifteen cents.

RIGHT: Caddo Parish's second courthouse on the public square in Shreveport was a Romanesque revival structure built in 1892. The United Daughters of the Confederacy erected the Confederate monument facing Texas Street in 1905. By 1918, when this photograph probably was taken, Milam Street, behind the courthouse, had already lost much of the residential appearance that it had retained into the twentieth century.

William Jennings Bryan spoke from the steps of this courthouse in 1900 when he campaigned unsuccessfully as the Democratic nominee for president.

Caddo Parish Court House

General Collection, LSUS Archives. Courtesy *River Cities* magazine.

The city fathers finally had had enough mud and dust by the mid-1890s to begin paving Shreveport's downtown streets. The work was slow, and bad weather often interrupted. Here crews lay bricks along Texas Street, *ca.* 1898.

Photograph by T. M. Elliott. Stockslager-Walters-Weaks Collection, LSUS Archives.

Prior to the disfranchising effects of the state constitution of 1898, blacks voted in significant numbers in Shreveport, as this photo- graph, taken on election day at the Caddo Parish Courthouse, re- veals. The date is about 1894.

General Collection, LSUS Archives.

In 1891 professional firemen took over from volunteer companies in Shreveport. The Fire Department counted six paid men and fifteen on call. It had three pieces of fire-fighting equipment, drawn by mules. To help in fighting fires, Shreveport had a city water system, which began operating under a privately held franchise in 1887. By the decade's end, the Fire Department had seventeen paid men, six mules, and two horses. Three of the firemen appear in the photograph above, *ca.* 1897.

Shreveport's Police Department (RIGHT) also achieved professional status during this period. Mayor E. R. Bernstein (on the far left in the front row, in civilian dress) poses with the city's finest in 1907.

65

Community Fair Collection, LSUS Archives. Donated by Mrs. J. Earl White.

Photograph by H. K. Vollrath. Community Fair Collection, LSUS Archives. Donated by Wade Hampton.

Shreveport enjoyed good rail connections, which ensured its continued importance as a center of commerce and population. The engine in this photograph from *ca.* 1900 is the KCS 103. The identities of the men are unknown, as is the reason why the boy is holding the shotgun.

Community Fair Collection, LSUS Archives. Donated by Mrs. Alton Waschka.

Meanwhile, some traffic continued to move at a more leisurely pace and with less commotion. Bert Stell and his horse Ray made deliveries in 1911 for Excelsior Laundry in Shreveport.

Samford C. Fullilove, Jr., Collection, LSUS Archives.

LEFT: Shreveport adopted the commission form of government in 1910. Members of the first commission were, *left to right,* W. S. Atkins, commissioner of streets and parks; S. C. Fullilove, commissioner of public safety; J. W. Eastham, mayor and commissioner of public affairs; C. W. Jack, city attorney; C. G. Rives, commissioner of accounts and finances; and John McCullough, commissioner of public utilities.

ABOVE: In 1911 the automobile still had not made a great difference in downtown Shreveport, as a view of Milam Street, looking east, reveals.

Henry Zwally's barbershop on Texas Street, *ca.* 1900, appears to have hired both whites and blacks. Although it is uncertain what jobs these black men performed, in the late nineteenth century there were many black barbers who had white customers.

Lewis W. Hine, a former schoolteacher in New York City and a self-taught photographer, used his camera to crusade for social reform. In 1908 he began helping the National Child Labor Committee to document abuses of children. His photographs from that period are famous, including those of "breakerboys" in mines, girls tending machinery in cotton mills, and children coping with life in the tenements.

Hine also photographed children employed as deliverers and newsboys. He found them wandering the streets as early as one or two o'clock in the morning. Sometimes small boys had to fend off hired bullies intent on chasing them away from their rounds.

RIGHT: Hine visited Shreveport in 1913, when he took this photograph of a fourteen-year-old boy who worked as a messenger for Western Union. "Says he goes to the Red Light District all the time," Hine reported.

Photograph by Lewis Hine. Courtesy of the Edward L. Bafford Photography Collection, Albin O. Kuhn Library and Gallery, University of Maryland Baltimore County.

LEFT: Hine found this jaunty young fellow in the heart of Shreveport's red-light district in St. Paul's Bottoms. The boy had just emerged from one of the brothels with the message that he holds in his right hand. "She gimme a quarter tip," he told the photographer.

RIGHT: This Hine subject was a thirteen-year-old boy who made deliveries for a drug company.

Photograph by Lewis Hine. Courtesy of the Edward L. Bafford Photography Collection, Albin O. Kuhn Library and Gallery, University of Maryland Baltimore County.

74

Shopping along Texas Street in 1906 might bring one past Charles Hoyer's grocery store at Texas and Edwards. Bananas and other fruits beckoned customers.

Liederkranz Hall, located at the corner of Pierre and Maple in Shreveport, was a center for recreation, where besides lifting a glass of beer one might play pool or bowl. This photograph was taken around 1905. Germans were the most numerous among Shreveport's foreign-born population in the late nineteenth century.

General Collection, LSUS Archives. Donated by Jack Barham.

Rendall Martin Collection, LSUS Archives.

LEFT: The Kirsch family in front of their home, *ca.* 1910. The house stood at 309 Edwards Street. With its turrets and gingerbread decoration, the Victorian structure came close to the middle-class ideal in this period. Shreveport had many such dwellings near its downtown, some designed by local architects, such as N. S. Allen.

ABOVE: Modest but functional was the home of the Henry Zwally family at 651 Olive Street, shown here as it appeared in 1911. The cistern next to the house caught rainwater, which families used for washing, bathing, and in some cases even drinking and cooking. By this time, the privately owned Shreveport Water Works Company supplied a reasonably pure product through its water system. This marked a great improvement, for cisterns might contain mosquito larvae and other foul objects. Worse were the shallow wells that some poorer families depended upon. Runoff from privies, stables, and other sources of pollution often contaminated such well water and contributed to disease.

Photograph by Shreveport Camera Club. Stockslager-Walters-Weaks Collection, LSUS Archives.

Spectators took naturally to horse racing, and not until professional baseball's rise was the sport of kings dethroned as Shreveport's most popular sport. Urban people knew horses and depended upon them, as did their rural counterparts, and appreciation for outstanding animals brought paying customers to the racetracks. Wagering was another attraction.

LEFT: "Hurdle racing" was popular at the track of the Shreveport Riding and Driving Club in the 1890s. The photograph dates from 1891. In 1906 the club's property became the home of the Louisiana State Fair, which used its racetrack and grandstand. That same year, automobiles raced, reaching speeds of twenty-five miles per hour.

RIGHT: Cycling was a more placid sport, though a fall might break one's bones. The rider is Marcus Jacobs of Shreveport as he appeared in 1888. Jacobs' bicycle attracted attention because of its unusual design: the small wheel is in front. Representative of the age's growing fascination with sports, the young man also pursued bowling, billiards, swimming, and skating.

OVERLEAF: In 1885 Shreveport fielded the O.K. Baseball Club, whose members proclaimed themselves "Champions of Louisiana Outside of New Orleans." These players are believed to be that team. By 1900 a professional team represented Shreveport in the Southern League. The city's ballpark could hold more than two thousand fans.

Interest in games did not stop with baseball. In 1902 the Shreveport Athletic Association fielded outstanding teams in football and track. Among the football team's vanquished opponents were Tulane and Louisiana State University. Performing before crowds at the state fair, the track team won the Southern Athletic Union championship in 1906.

Benjamin Jacobs Collection, LSUS Archives. Donated by Mr. and Mrs. Philip Haglund.

Community Fair Collection, LSUS Archives. Donated by First National Bank, Shreveport.

Tennis was a genteel diversion for both sexes. Here members of
the Minden Tennis Club pose for the photographer in 1891.

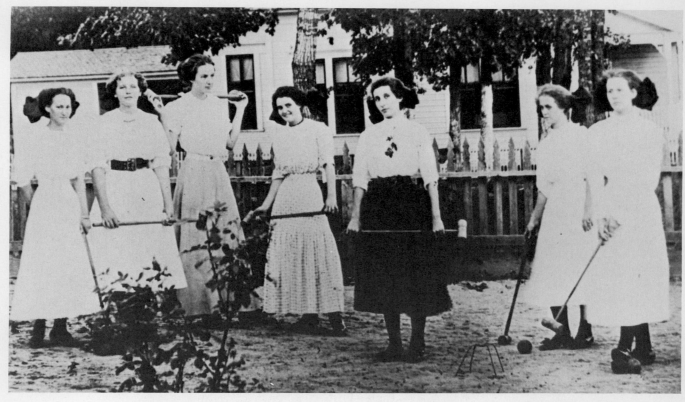

Community Fair Collection, LSUS Archives. Donated by Mrs. Julius Horton.

One's yard could support a game of croquet, such as this match in Vivian, *ca.* 1915. The players are, *left to right,* Mrs. J. D. Beaseley, Myrtis Hughes Reed, Estelle Van Horn, Gertrude Lee Pardue, Esther Beddingfield, Josie Graham, and Vivian Galloway. The J. D. Beaseley home is in the background.

RIGHT: Despite interest in sports, the idea of leisure itself took a long time to take hold. Most families did not take vacations, for example. Resorts that prospered, such as Hot Springs, Arkansas, often did so because they advertised themselves as centers for restoring health and vigor. Thus, a few hours stolen here and there often sufficed for relaxation, such as this outing on Old River. A member of the Shreveport Camera Club took this photograph around 1896. The man in front is Kirby Chase Guynemere.

Photograph by Shreveport Camera Club. N. S. Allen Collection, LSUS Archives. Donated by Colonel and Mrs. Robert Webb.

JOY RIDING AT THE STATE FAIR. SHREVEPORT. LA.

Community Fair Collection, LSUS Archives. Donated by Jack Norman.

LEFT: "Joy riding" was more of a novelty than a popular pastime when this serious trio posed for a portrait at the Louisiana State Fair, *ca.* 1910. Most people had to marvel at someone else's automobile rather than enjoy one of their own. The automobile's potential for inspiring envy led President Woodrow Wilson of Princeton University to warn in 1906, "Nothing has spread socialistic feeling in this country more than the use of the automobile." By 1915 the Caddo Parish sheriff's office had registered nearly five hundred automobiles.

ABOVE: One enthusiastic motorist was Henry Carlton, shown taking some female friends for a spin in Shreveport, *ca.* 1903. Carlton, a cotton broker, had a reputation as the city's most eligible bachelor.

Photograph by J. C. Ewing. Louisiana State Fair Collection, LSUS Archives.

Two views taken from a panoramic photograph offer glimpses of the Louisiana State Fair in Shreveport in 1910. For those who preferred not to eat in the Peerless Dining Room, there was the Christian Ladies Lunch Room.

Shreveport's first state fair, located between Pierre Avenue and Jordan Street, went broke during the depression in 1894. Its successor, organized in 1906, took over the grounds of the old Shreveport Riding and Driving Club. Among the fair's earliest themes

Photograph by J. C. Ewing. Louisiana State Fair Collection, LSUS Archives.

was agricultural diversification, which the boll weevil helped to inspire. In 1910 the fair also began a campaign to promote better methods for raising livestock. The organizers set apart a "Negro Day" for teaching progressive farming methods to blacks. A spe-cial building housed exhibits from the black population. In 1912 the fair's association deeded its property to the city of Shreveport but retained the privilege of using the land and buildings thirty days a year.

Webster Fair Collection, LSUS Archives. Donated by Lillian Willis.

These young gentlemen from Minden created their own musical entertainment, *ca.* 1900. Concerts by amateur groups were popular, and public events often called for musicians' participation.

Alfred Flournoy, Jr., Collection, LSUS Archives.

For many years, Shreveport emulated New Orleans by having Mardi Gras celebrations. Here some laborers appear to be oblivious to the decorated carriages passing by, part of a Mardi Gras parade, *ca*. 1900. The young woman on the left in the buggy is Theo Minge. Beside her is Gilpin Flournoy.

The Hutchinson family of Caspiana return from an outing with stringers of bream, *ca.* 1900. Fishing was an acceptable sport for women, so long as they went properly dressed. A bonnet to shade a lady's delicate face from the sun was standard.

Hunters from Webster Parish take advantage of the snow, which permitted them to track down rabbits and other game, *ca.* 1910.

Community Fair Collection, LSUS Archives. Donated by Mrs. Olin Oden.

Piling into a surrey behind a gentle horse could be great fun, particularly if a photographer was waiting to take your picture. *Ca.* 1899.

The girl's name is Saidie. Her rabbit's name is Burnie. Shreveport, *ca*. 1900.

Community Fair Collection, LSUS Archives. Donated by Clara Bryan.

LEFT: Young women. Shreveport, *ca.* 1900.

RIGHT: Mr. and Mrs. A. M. Solley and daughters, of Vivian, *ca.* 1895.

Community Fair Collection, LSUS Archives. Donated by Mrs. Julius L. Horton.

Josie Carter of Shreveport, *ca.* 1897. She married W. K. Henderson, Jr., who became nationally famous through his anti–chain
store crusades over KWKH Radio.

Community Fair Collection, LSUS Archives. Donated by Mrs. Olin Oden.

The two boys with the tricycle are Walter and Arthur Hawkins of East Point, in Red River Parish, *ca*. 1900.

Photograph by Joe Dambly. Community Fair Collection, LSUS Archives. Donated by Mrs. L. H. Crook.

H. C. Teacle appeared ready for play when he posed for Joe Dambly's camera in Shreveport, *ca*. 1905. Teacle grew up to become vice-president of First National Bank of Shreveport.

LEFT: The white boy is Floyd Williams. The name of the black child is unknown. Caddo Parish, *ca.* 1900.

Community Fair Collection, LSUS Archives. Donated by Mrs. Julius L. Horton.

Photograph by T. H. Elliott. Community Fair Collection, LSUS Archives. Donated by Clara Bryan.

These young women attended the Kate P. Nelson Seminary in Shreveport, *ca*. 1895. The gentleman may be a professor. Miss Nelson established her school, which she first called the Shreveport Seminary, in the old Battle house on Edwards Street. Later, after a move to the Ardis house, the school's growing number of students required construction of a larger building at Texas and Grand. Many of the school's alumnae became teachers.

ABOVE: Female members of the Stringfellow family and a servant. Shreveport, *ca.* 1900.

RIGHT: Ewald Hoyer, the first mayor of Bossier City, is on the right in this photograph. Posing with him, *ca.* 1907, are his three brothers. They are, *from left,* Hugo, Charles, and Gus Hoyer.

Hoyer Family Collection, LSUS Archives. Donated by Charles Tubbs.

Hoyer Family Collection, LSUS Archives. Donated by Charles Tubbs.

Community Fair Collection, LSUS Archives. Donated by Mrs. Olin Oden.

LEFT: Elsie Hoyer of Bossier Parish, *ca.* 1900.

ABOVE: John Sibley of Caddo Parish, *ca.* 1900.

Conductors for Shreveport's new electric streetcars, *ca.* 1896. *Front row: left,* Dosh Clanton; *right,* H. H. Lawsford; *back row: left,* a Mr. McNorton; *right,* Jim Monzinger.

Pearl Dillon, daughter of William F. and Pearl Jacobs Dillon of Shreveport, is dressed up for a trip to the photographer's studio, *ca.* 1905.

Tom and Cora Amiss, with attendants, on their wedding day.
Shreveport, *ca.* 1906.

Stockslager-Walters-Weaks Collection, LSUS Archives.

Three generations of the Weaks family of Shreveport, *ca.* 1905.

Part II
The Modern Years

PEACE! declared the Shreveport *Journal* on November 11, 1918. The Great War was over, and people in Shreveport had been deliriously celebrating since 1:59 that morning when the newspaper editors got word from the Associated Press and alerted the Fire Department to sound the signal.

Thousands who had been waiting for the armistice took to the streets. They cheered, sang, blew car horns, even shot off guns. The El Karubah band, which had been on standby, marched through the downtown, stopping at the Youree and Inn hotels to give patriotic concerts. There throngs of emotional people sang the "Star Spangled Banner" and the "Marseillaise."

At last, Shreveport could return to "normalcy," as President Harding would describe the postwar decade. There would be peace, prosperity, and progress. These were noble goals for any period, but at the end of World War I, Americans felt especially justified in expressing their good cheer. They had helped to save democracy, and now they wanted to reward themselves.

Shreveport appears to have embraced the spirit of these "ballyhoo years" in a way that almost caricatured the 1920s. The city's newspapers and its commercial-civic elite preached the gospel of business, and boosters predicted glorious achievements for the New South. Said the Shreveport *Times* in a tone typical of the editorial pages of the city's two daily newspapers: "Shreveport is one of the most remarkable cities of the country. . . . When fully awake there will be a wonderful development which will shatter our present boasted records." [1]

In fact, these were good years for many who shared the city's growing affluence. Railroads had guaranteed Shreveport's importance as a regional center, and the downtown's humming activity reflected an economic base of agriculture, petroleum, light manufacturing, and timber. Rising property values in the central district caused residences to give way to tall new commercial buildings. Meanwhile, streets that had been paved only a generation before became choked with automobile traffic, signaling the decline of the streetcar's importance. "Shreveport: See It Grow Day by Day" was the title of a regular front-page feature in the Shreveport *Times,* and slick promotional material from the chamber of commerce and other groups helped to proclaim the "Gospel of Shreveport." Evidence of the city's growth came in the census figures: Shreveport's population jumped from 28,015 in 1910 to 43,874 by 1920. For the first time, urban dwellers in Caddo Parish outnumbered their rural

1. Shreveport *Times*, March 25, 1923.

counterparts. A decade later, the city's population would be 76,655.[2]

Like many southern cities, Shreveport stretched its boundaries in the 1920s. Annexation of Agurs in 1926 and South Highlands and Cedar Grove a year later gave "Greater Shreveport" an area of almost twenty square miles by 1931, in contrast to the settlement in 1839 that included slightly less than one square mile. New neighborhoods grew up. Thanks to the automobile, they were not so restricted as before by proximity to streetcar lines. Here and elsewhere, the automobile gradually began to shift the focus of the city outward to the suburbs, which became more independent and more segregated by class and race. The immediate impact, however, was to bring pressure for improvements downtown, where motorists clogged streets with their vehicles and competed for scarce parking. By 1927 Shreveport had 111 miles of paved streets and alleys. Downtown, there was a new traffic-light system to relieve congestion of automobiles. Twenty "white ways" aided travelers at night, as did the more than 3,000 incandescent arc lights scattered throughout the rest of the city. Shreveport's first zoning ordinance, adopted in 1925, sought to regulate growth, though city officials admitted that there were many difficulties with this new concept and few precedents.[3]

Progressive city officials, typified by Mayor L. E. Thomas, campaigned for improved public services to catch up with the city's growth and to meet rising expectations of citizens. The city government built new parks and a small nine-hole golf course. The parish finally got a public library in 1923, after a long period of frustration following the public's rejection of a Carnegie library twenty years earlier. Among the first books collected were 7,188 volumes from a small library that a group of local women had operated in the parish courthouse. In 1925 the parish school board opened C. E. Byrd High School, and three years later it added Fair Park High. Both were for white students. Blacks, meanwhile, continued to attend Central Colored High School. For students interested in higher education, there was Centenary College, which in 1908 had accepted the Shreveport Progressive League's invitation to move to the city and occupy a forty-acre site donated by a local real estate firm. Under leadership of President George S. Sexton, who had been pastor of the First Methodist Church of Shreveport, the little college added new buildings and increased enrollment during the 1920s.[4]

The city secured a reliable water source in 1926 with construction of a dam where the Kansas City Southern Railroad

2. *Ibid.*, March 27, 1923; U.S. Bureau of the Census, *1980 Census of Population: Number of Inhabitants*, I, 177.

3. Shreveport *Times* (centennial edition), June 28, 1935; Barth, *City People*, 8, 57; Brownell, "The Urban South Comes of Age," 135, 155–56; *Biennial Report of the Mayor and Commissioners of the City of Shreveport for the Years 1925 and 1926* (Shreveport, 1927), 24, 54, 91, 122–24. Complaints about Shreveport's congested traffic were commonplace until

construction of the interstate system through the city. One problem was that Highway 80 went through the downtown.

4. *Biennial Report of the Mayor and Commissioners for 1925 and 1926*, p. 97; Maude Hearn O'Pry, *Chronicles of Shreveport* (Shreveport, 1928), 288–89; Mary Lilla McLure, *History of Shreveport and Shreveport Builders* (2 vols; Shreveport 1937, 1951), I, 163–64; Walter Lowery, "Centenary College of Louisiana, 1825–1975," Shreveport *Times*, February 11, 1975.

tracks spanned Cross Bayou. This turned the old bed of Cross Lake, which had drained after the removal of the log-jams in the Red River, into a reservoir eight miles long and from one to three miles wide. For this project and other additions to the city's water and sewage system, voters had approved overwhelmingly in 1923 the issuance of a million dollars in bonds. The addition of the reservoir, with its capacity of twenty billion gallons, resolved festering problems with the city's water source and guaranteed sufficient capacity for many decades of growth. Officials also launched such public projects as the Market Street viaduct and the Municipal Memorial Auditorium. Meanwhile the downtown's skyline changed with construction of the Slattery Building and the new parish courthouse. Local newspaper editors and other founts of opinion floridly touted these developments as a natural progression toward the city's modern destiny. Their language confirmed one journalist's observation that the average southerner "is a born booster, and the mood is contagious."[5]

In 1929 voters approved a plan to build an airport near the downtown, in Bossier Parish. They also approved the purchase of twenty-two thousand acres of land in Bossier that would become the site of the United States Army's Barksdale Field. An error committed when clerks recorded enabling legislation for this cross-parish transaction gave Governor Huey P. Long a political opening in a feud that he was

waging with officials in Caddo Parish. In return for his support, Long demanded that the school board of Caddo Parish accept his program to provide free textbooks to schoolchildren and withdraw its suit that challenged the constitutionality of that program. The state had set up depositories to give away textbooks near the parish depositories that sold them. Thus, students could either buy their books or get them free. Long further demanded more support from the Caddo Parish legislative delegation and an apology from the Shreveport Chamber of Commerce for having resisted his textbook program. The governor got his wishes.[6]

It is not surprising that Shreveport's business-oriented progressives resisted much of Long's popular program, even to the point of looking silly over the textbook issue. Southern progressives during this period were successful in promoting economic growth and efficient government. Paved roads, good schools, elimination of wasteful spending, business expansion—these conformed to their idea of progress. Their conservatism, however, often made them indifferent to such maladies as racism and maldistribution of wealth and political power. Some were also simply profoundly suspicious of democracy. Governor John M. Parker, considered Louisiana's quintessential progressive, had only contempt for professional politicians, preferring to leave government in the hands of a well-meaning elite.[7]

5. Lowin Humphrey, "A History of Cross Lake, 1883–1926," *North Louisiana Historical Association Journal*, X (Summer, 1979), 91–92, 94; George Brown Tindall, *The Emergence of the New South, 1913–1945* (Baton Rouge, 1967), 98.

6. Tom Ruffin, "The Textbook Trauma, Part I: The Long Year," *Shreveport Magazine*, XXXIII (August, 1978), 30–32, 72–82, and "Part II: Within or Without," *Shreveport Magazine*, XXXIII (September, 1978), 26–28, 46–53.

7. Tindall, *The Emergence of the New South*, 223–24, 233; Matthew

Increasing segregation coincided with a migration of blacks that began around World War I. Regionwide, this set into motion millions of people, taking them from farms to nearby cities and then often to the great northern metropolises. Discrimination in housing pushed blacks into inner-city neighborhoods, usually on less desirable land. In Shreveport, St. Paul's Bottoms, a low-lying area just west of the downtown, became an almost entirely black neighborhood except for white prostitutes who worked there until World War II. Landlords doubled the density of housing, sometimes cramming twenty-four shotguns into a single block. Black housing in Shreveport was vastly inferior to white. City records of 1925 put the average cost of a new "Negro dwelling" at $895; that of a new "white dwelling" was $4,567.[8]

Along with losing their voting rights in the 1890s, blacks also lost economic power. Good jobs, for the most part, went to whites, while blacks swelled the ranks of the unskilled, low-paid workers. Nevertheless, some blacks managed by catering to other blacks. They ran funeral homes, grocery stores, and other businesses and offered professional services. Booker T. Washington's philosophy of racial accommodation was popular among those blacks who aspired to join the middle class. Black leaders campaigned to bring better public services to their neighborhoods, which white politicians often neglected.[9]

The center of black commerce and society in Shreveport during the first half of the twentieth century was a three-block stretch on the outskirts of the downtown along Texas Avenue. There doctors and other black professionals had their offices. Black-owned drugstores, barbershops, cleaners, pool halls, cafes, newspapers, insurance companies, and other businesses operated on "the Avenue," sometimes alongside those owned by Italians, Jews, Chinese, Lebanese, and Syrians. Among black undertakers on the Avenue was J. S. Williams, who established one of the city's most influential black families. And *Who's Who in Colored Louisiana* reported in the 1930s, "N.O. may be the biggest city in the state, but the best colored lawyer is in Shreveport." It referred to Charles Roberson, who had practiced for twenty years on the Avenue. In 1920 Melvin L. Collins founded his weekly newspaper, the Shreveport *Sun,* which went on to become a lasting and important voice for blacks. Also on the Avenue, four black fraternal organizations had established headquarters by 1925. One of them, the four-story temple of the Grand Court Order of Calanthe, had a rooftop ballroom.[10]

Meanwhile blacks secured further opportunities for education in 1917 with the opening of Central Colored High. Initially, there were ten teachers and ten grades, and Central drew many of its students from rural schools within the parish. Sometimes students would board with families in town. Rural black schools had from one to three teachers each, and supplies were chronically short. In 1927 the school board moved the elementary grades at Central to West

---

J. Schott, "Progressives Against Democracy: Electoral Reform in Louisiana, 1894–1921," *Louisiana History,* XX (1979), 258–59.

8. Arnold (ed.), *St. Paul's Bottoms to Ledbetter Heights; Biennial Report of the Mayor and Commissioners for 1925 and 1926,* p. 50.

9. Rabinowitz, "Southern Urban Development," 117–18; Brownell, "The Urban South Comes of Age," 139–40.

10. Chris Sherman, "On the Avenue: Where Black Louisiana Danced Under the Stars," Shreveport *Journal,* February 22, 1984.

Shreveport School. In 1950 Central became a junior high school when the school board opened Booker T. Washington High.[11]

White minority groups in Shreveport also encountered discrimination, but it was a more subtle variety than that experienced by blacks. Newly arriving Italians, for example, were set apart by their foreign language and culture. Shreveport's Italian community centered itself in the Allendale and West End sections, where it promoted self-pride through an Italian language newspaper and the Italia Moderna Society. Many Italian families operated small grocery stores and depended heavily upon black customers. Often these families lived behind or above their businesses.[12]

Jews came to Shreveport early: as many as a dozen families lived in the city by 1848. Many acquired property and social status. By 1900 there were more than a hundred Jewish families, most of whom were members of the Reform congregation. In 1902 adherents of the Orthodox wing of Judaism formed a second congregation. Jews were active politically; three from their community were among the early mayors of Shreveport. Jewish families also rose to prominence in business and the professions. A. D. and Julian Saenger, for example, began the Saenger Amusement Company over their drugstore at Louisiana and Milam streets. The company grew into an international chain of

some three hundred movie theaters. Its flagship was the magnificent neobaroque Strand Theatre, built in 1925 at Crockett and Louisiana streets. Among distinguished Jewish physicians were Dr. Jacob Bodenheimer, president of the Shreveport Medical Society in 1920, and Dr. A. A. Herold, Sr., president of the Louisiana State Medical Society in 1927. Shreveport avoided anti-Semitism in most of its uglier forms, even during the 1920s when Jews faced increased discrimination in America. One explanation is that Jews were in the city virtually from the beginning. Thus, there was less tendency to look upon Jewish families as dangerous outsiders. Also, the Reform tradition minimized cultural differences with Christians.[13]

Still, there were occasional incidents in which conformity to Christian practices ignored Jewish sentiment. One led to a famous case before the Louisiana Supreme Court in 1915. The Caddo Parish Board of School Directors had requested that teachers and principals open the public schools every day with readings from the Bible. The board further decreed that "when the leader is willing to do so," the Lord's Prayer would be offered. Among the three plaintiffs who sued the board over its policy was a Jewish attorney from Shreveport named Sidney L. Herold. Earlier, he had entered a suit against mandatory reading of the Bible in Pennsylvania's schools. In its decision, the court held that officials in Caddo Parish had acted improperly. It was impossible to read from the New Testament without giving instruction in Christianity, and that discriminated against Jews. As for the

11. Diane Hollenshead, "Central: School Gave Blacks a Chance for Diploma" and "Glory Days of BTW: School Once Featured in *Life* Magazine," both in Shreveport *Journal*, February 22, 1984.

12. Interview with Frank Fulco by Bailey Thomson, August 15, 1980. Fulco was publisher of Shreveport's *Italia Moderna* newspaper. He served on the Caddo Parish Police Jury and later in the Louisiana Legislature.

13. Beverly S. Williams, "Anti-Semitism and Shreveport, Louisiana: The Situation in the 1920s," *Louisiana History,* XXI (1980), 389–94, 396; *B'Nai Zion: One Hundred Years* (Shreveport, 1970?).

school board's argument that teachers could simply excuse children who did not wish to participate in the Bible readings and prayer, the court said: "The exclusion of a pupil under such circumstances puts him in a class by himself; it subjects him to religious stigma; and all because of his religious belief. Equality in education would be destroyed by such an act, under a Constitution which seeks to establish equality and freedom in religious matters. The Constitution forbids that this shall be done."[14]

Southern cities could be strange mixtures of puritanism and hedonism. In Shreveport, "The City of Churches," one saw this phenomenon in the toleration of an official red-light, or "segregated," district in St. Paul's Bottoms. Indeed, one account of the district's history declares that prostitution was a major industry, claiming there were some sixty bawdy houses within the legal zone. Here men went seeking not only sexual pleasures but also bootleg booze and gambling. Country boys attending the state fair were warned to stay clear of the district's moral pitfalls, though many of them found the painted women to be more alluring than the agricultural exhibits.[15]

After the United States entered World War I, representatives for the Council of National Defense declared Shreveport's vice district to be the largest for any city of its size in the country. It would not do to locate a training camp nearby. The council also expressed concern for the service men passing through, who might be exposed to venereal disease. There followed a campaign to clean up the district and end the embarrassment for the city's progressive image. With the Rotary Club leading and the churches offering strong support, the reformers forced an election on November 15, 1917, and won approval of an ordinance to shut down the bawdy houses. VICE DISTRICT VOTED OUT, reported the Shreveport *Times*. "The lights will go out, the quarter-in-the-slot pianos will be still, and no more will be heard the abandoned laugh or vituperous tongue of the scarlet woman."[16] Actually, the prostitutes returned after a while, and a new "segregated district" operated quite brazenly until authorities shut it down in 1941.

A black teen-ager who performed on the corners in the red-light district went on to become the legendary Leadbelly of the blues. Huddie Ledbetter was born in rural Caddo Parish in 1889. By the time he was sixteen, according to his recollections, he already was visiting the brothels along Fannin Street. His blues singing and guitar playing carried him to roadhouses, where on one occasion he had his throat slit and on another he killed a man in an argument over a woman. He did time for the murder in a Texas prison. John and Alan Lomax, who were traveling the back roads of the South in search of folk talent, discovered Ledbetter in the Louisiana State Penitentiary at Angola, where he was serving another sentence for an attempted murder. "We

14. *Herold* et al. v. *Parish Board of School Directors* et al., Supreme Court of Louisiana, March 22, 1915 (136 La. 1034). The United States Supreme Court cited the Herold case in 1963 when the majority on the court ruled that similar devotional exercises in public schools in Pennsylvania were unconstitutional. Many of the arguments that the Louisiana court addressed in the Herold decision continue to be raised nationwide, as various groups and politicians seek to circumvent the U.S. Supreme Court's prohibition against state-sponsored prayers in the public schools.

15. Stuck, *Annie McCune*, 85, 89–90.

16. *Ibid.*, 86–89, 93–95, 97.

were deeply moved by the flawless tenor voice which rang out across the cotton field like a big sweet-toned trumpet," Alan Lomax recalled. "We believed Leadbelly when he said, 'I'ze the king of all the 12-string guitar players in the world.'" Governor O. K. Allen had Ledbetter released into the custody of the Lomaxes in 1934, and they brought him to New York City. There and on college campuses his original though unpolished style drew appreciative audiences until his death in 1949. Among the hundreds of Ledbetter's compositions that made him an important transitional figure between black blues and modern pop music were "Cotton Fields," "Irene Goodnight," "The Midnight Special," and an allegedly autobiographical piece called "Fannin Street."[17]

Profound tensions underlay the 1920s, as changes in values and manners collided with tradition. In 1920 the city underwent a bout of anti-unionism, inspired in part by a great nationwide scare over political radicalism, which in the wake of the Bolsheviks' victory in Russia appeared to threaten the West. REDS PLAN TO TOUCH TORCH TO WORLD screamed a headline in the Shreveport Times on September 6, 1920. There was nothing in the activities of the local unions to suggest any sympathy for communism. Indeed, unions had shown a consistent conservatism on such matters as patriotism, the work ethic, and prevailing moral standards. In 1905 the carpenters' local had refused to endorse the socialist Eugene Debs for president. Nevertheless, some advertisements in local papers tied unionism to bolshevism. Unions came under direct attack from the Shreveport Open Shop Committee, which was formed in October, 1920. The committee's leadership, drawn from business, education, the churches, and other segments of the established order, promoted the open shop as the "American Plan," a tactic fostered by the National Association of Manufacturers and the National Chamber of Commerce. The unions fought back in this propaganda war as best they could in advertisements and flyers of their own. The battle did not peter out until the end of the decade.[18]

A more lasting concern of the 1920s, however, was the challenge to conventional morality, which shook the foundation of the ideal Victorian home. Again, the automobile was an agent of change. It provided young people with a way to escape the cloying supervision of their parents, and more than a few defenders of decency saw a correlation between automobiles and the enthusiasm for cosmetics and dancing in roadhouses. In their famous sociological study *Middletown,* the Lynds quoted a judge who declared the automobile to be a veritable "house of prostitution on wheels." Many prayer meetings were given over to warnings about the relationship between backseat petting and the heat of hell's fire.

As a consequence, the period saw greater emphasis on regulating behavior. In Shreveport, records for 1925–1926 show 246 arrests for violation of the "moral code," 564 arrests for vagrancy (usually applied to unemployed blacks), 1,714 arrests for being drunk and disorderly, 614 arrests for liquor law violations, and 652 arrests for gambling with dice. By contrast, there were only 19 arrests in those

17. Phil Martin, " 'Leadbelly': A Dangerous Man with a Gift for Singing, Playing the Blues," Shreveport *Journal,* February 22, 1984.

18. Humphreys, "A History of the Shreveport Carpenters," 5, 9–11.

years for burglary and larceny, and 37 for breaking and entering, which indicates that the number of reported crimes against property was low. There was 1 arrest for possession of marijuana. In 1926 the Police Department added four deputies, and it reported "wonderful results in the way of catching bootleggers and all other classes of criminals."[19]

The Ku Klux Klan was among groups that advocated tighter restrictions on behavior. It enjoyed a national resurgence in the 1920s, capitalizing on anxiety over modern challenges to old-time religion and traditional values. In fundamentalist Shreveport, a powerful Klan chapter grew up, proclaiming its devotion to Protestant, native-born Americans and to right living. Along with the city's blacks, Jews and Catholics came under suspicion. More important, Klan members used violence and threats to attack bootlegging, prostitution, joyriding, and other "immorality." For a while, local citizens hailed the chapter as their protector, and at its height membership numbered about 4,500. The Klan chapter endorsed public candidates, such as L. E. Thomas for mayor, and it supported local charitable efforts. Its public initiation ceremonies and cross-burning rallies attracted enormous crowds, who on several occasions heard Dr. E. W. Evans, the Klan's imperial wizard.[20] Nationwide, public relations turned the Klan into a paying proposition.

19. *Biennial Report of the Mayor and Commissioners for 1925 and 1926*, pp. 38–40.
20. Frank Granger, "Reaction to Change: The Ku Klux Klan in Shreveport, 1920–1929," *North Louisiana Historical Association Journal*, IX (Fall, 1978), 220–24.

Many a kleagle and grand goblin got a cut from the annual dues of ten dollars per member.

Following a sensational murder and trial in Mer Rouge, which involved the Morehouse Parish Klan, more opponents of the secret organization spoke out, including the Shreveport *Times*. The newspaper joined Governor Parker and other officials in calling for laws that would require Klan members to remove their masks and register their organization. The paper also sought to reduce the Klan's political influence. An editorial in 1923, for example, praised a young candidate for the Legislature after he publicly disavowed any connection to the Klan in response to charges by a New Orleans paper. The *Times* criticized certain candidates for not being more forthright about the issue. Around 1924 the Shreveport Klan slipped into decline, as a new state law unmasked the membership and public interest waned. By 1927 the organization's functions were reduced to poorly attended parades and watermelon parties.[21]

A fierce reaction against modernism took place also in certain churches. Sometimes popular fads were the source of anger, as in 1923 when authorities broke up a marathon dance at Cedar Grove after church members in the area complained. Most of those taking part cooled their heels immediately, but ten couples boarded a streetcar and continued dancing. When last seen, they were headed for Bossier Parish. Churches in the city strove to compete with the new entertainments. On Easter Sunday, 1923, they called for 100 percent attendance. "The Easter invitation of the

21. *Ibid.*, 223–25; Shreveport *Times*, December 26, 1923.

churches of Shreveport should be accepted gratefully by the people of this city and vicinity," advised the *Times*.[22]

Despite challenges to tradition, the 1920s were inclined toward complacency and conformity. Few people dared to espouse liberal ideas, for fear of being labeled a radical. And if some church leaders bravely championed racial justice and the social gospel, others declared that Christianity was much like business or the Rotary Club. In his best-selling book of the period, *The Man Nobody Knows,* Bruce Barton proclaimed Jesus Christ to have been the world's first great salesman. Business itself became a kind of national religion during the Coolidge presidency, and Shreveport's boosters worshiped at the altar as true believers.

Among quiet changes occurring in the workplace, however, was a rise in the number of working women—something seldom mentioned in the booster literature. By the 1920s, women were working in offices and factories. Meanwhile they drew support from women's church groups and suffrage organizations that campaigned for shorter working hours for women and reform of child labor practices. The new working woman, often self-supporting and independent, clashed dramatically with the older ideal of the mother in the home. At the same time, female workers were important to the South's industrialization. Here was a dilemma for conservative males.

The years between the wars were not all business. There was also fun, including new entertainment. Radio became first a novelty and then a necessity. Listeners strained to follow the great events of the day, and entertainers gained national audiences. Near Shreveport, at his country place, which he called Kennonwood, W. K. Henderson, Jr., operated one of the nation's first clear-channel stations. The relaxed style of "Old Man Henderson" and his crusade against grocery-store chains were familiar to millions, who would tune in to hear him proclaim: "Hello—World! Hello, you li'l ole doggone North American continent!" (Walter Winchell would later use a similar opening line.) Then he would launch into advocating his various causes. His wars with the Department of Commerce over regulation of air waves inspired the creation of the Federal Radio Commission.[23]

Largely due to improved communications, sports became a passion. When Shreveport's baseball fans were not watching the local Gassers or some amateur team play, they were turning to radio and the newspapers to follow their favorite major league teams. Centenary College in Shreveport found that it could rouse support by having successful football teams, and it inaugurated competition with nationally ranked powerhouses. At first, local citizens paid the team's expenses, a loose arrangement that brought condemnation—perhaps hypocritically—from other colleges. President Sexton corrected this practice, thereby saving the football program.[24]

22. *Ibid.*, June 26, March 23, 1923.

23. Lillian Jones Hall, "A Historical Study of Programming Techniques and Practices of Radio Station KWKH, Shreveport, Louisiana, 1922–1950" (Ph.D. dissertation, Louisiana State University, 1959), 29–44; Shreveport *Times* (centennial edition), June 28, 1935; Tindall, *Emergence of the New South,* 595.

24. Lowery, "Centenary College of Louisiana."

The city became more serious about its cultural offerings. On December 22, 1922, the Shreveport Little Theatre offered its first play, *Suppressed Desires,* in the auditorium at city hall. Three years earlier, organizers had formed the Women's Department Club, which they dedicated to improving Shreveport's social and cultural life. In 1923 the club broke ground for a handsome two-story brick building at Line and Margaret. There artists performed and scholars lectured. In some cases attendance of these highbrow events was worth credit from Centenary.[25] For less sophisticated tastes, there were local marching bands and radio performers, some of the latter affecting a hillbilly manner.

A remarkable creativity appeared in the city's architecture. Sam G. Wiener, among others, worked brilliantly in the new styles, principally art deco and international. Among his prizes were the Municipal Memorial Auditorium (1929), his home at 615 Longleaf Road (1937), and the city's incinerator (1935), the latter of which the federal government's Works Progress Administration financed. The architectural firm of Edward F. Neild and Dewey Somdal produced another fine example of art deco in the design of the State Fair Exhibit Museum (1939). Earlier, the firm had mixed art deco and classical features in designing the Caddo Parish Courthouse (1928). Harry S. Truman made Neild a consulting architect on projects to build courthouses in Kansas City and Independence, Missouri. After he became president, Truman appointed Neild to be the architect for reconstruction of the White House. Later, after he had left office, Truman called upon Neild again—this time to design the Truman Library in Independence.

As the 1920s closed, cities such as Shreveport seemed to be enjoying phenomenal progress. In part, this was true, because they had started so far behind their northern counterparts. White-collar jobs continued to predominate in Shreveport's local economy, though manufacturing had increased significantly since the turn of the century. In the agricultural hinterland, meanwhile, farmers suffered from overproduction and low prices. For many of them, hard times had begun in the early 1920s. Still, the period of the 1920s deserved much of its reputation for good times. The years from about World War I until 1930 saw enough of peace and prosperity to permit many people to enjoy life more and to conclude that things were getting better.

Such optimism died hard, even as the Great Depression wore on. For one thing, Shreveport escaped for the most part the demoralizing effects of bank failures. For another, the city's local economy got what amounted to a new industry in the army's Barksdale Field, which was dedicated in 1933. Also, in the mid- to late 1930s extensive development occurred in the great East Texas oil and gas fields. Deep wells tapped some of the largest pools of crude known to exist at that time. Money from the exploitation of this resource flowed back into Shreveport. Caddo Parish's own fields produced 19,187,884 barrels of oil in 1937 and 78,374,834 cubic feet of gas.[26]

25. McLure, *History of Shreveport and Shreveport Builders,* 177, 207–208.

26. "Composite Report on Shreveport-Minden, Louisiana War Production Area; Caddo, Bossier, and Webster Parishes," Office of Defense, Health and Welfare Sources, Region X, San Antonio, Texas, and National Resources Planning Board, Region V, Dallas, Texas (1942), 5, LSUS Ar-

In the middle of the depression, Shreveport celebrated its centennial. Organizers chose 1935 as the year for the event, to commemorate the signing of a treaty one hundred years earlier in which the Caddo Indians had ceded their lands to the federal government, thereby opening up Northwest Louisiana to settlement. There may also have been a desire to capitalize on the excitement that was building for the centennial of the Texas Revolution, which was to be celebrated in 1936 in Dallas. During the week of activities, which began with a parade on June 29, hardly a waking hour passed without some program, concert, play, or reenactment. Months of work went into the planning, and committees counted long lists of participants. The city's two dailies published huge special editions filled with valuable, though occasionally hyperbolic and exaggerated, accounts of the area's history and accomplishments. Thus, one could read that Shreveport "has reached in all things the known heights of modern urban development and on the whole its people are prosperous and happy."[27]

Perhaps the times themselves demanded an unflinching boosterism, for the news from abroad in 1935 was not good. The Nazis in Germany pressed ahead with plans for rearmament. They tightened their control domestically through oppressive new directives, including policies that suggested the new order to come. The Italians and the Japanese also continued to build up their military strength.

In Baton Rouge, meanwhile, Senator Huey P. Long tightened his control of state politics as he prepared to challenge Franklin D. Roosevelt for the presidency. Not surprisingly, enemies of the Kingfish compared his ruthless methods with those of Hitler and Mussolini. Shreveport's establishment lined up against Long while he was still governor. Mayor Thomas, members of Caddo Parish's school board, and others, for example, sought unsuccessfully to block the administration's program to distribute free school books in the parish. Long's assassination on September 8, 1935, did not end the political struggles, and the state's conservative anti-Long faction continued to oppose the Long machine that carried on in the Kingfish's absence.

A native of Winn Parish, Long had practiced law in Shreveport prior to winning the governorship. Gerald L. K. Smith, the lieutenant whom Long entrusted to lead his Share Our Wealth program, also had lived in the city, arriving in 1929 from Indiana, where he had been a member of the Klan. Smith served as pastor of the Kings Highway Christian Church until 1933. In Shreveport he plunged into community activities that ranged from managing the community chest drive to organizing lumber workers into a union and criticizing sweatshops and debt peonage. He could deliver a thundering sermon without prior preparation, a talent that served him well in politics. H. L. Mencken remarked that Smith was the greatest speaker he had ever heard. At Long's funeral, Smith delivered the eulogy. He broke with the senator's political heirs soon afterward and left Louisiana in 1935. Later, he turned to anti-Semitism and other causes of the extreme right.[28]

---

chives. The parish's lumber industry remained important as well, producing 19,397,454 board feet in 1936. Meanwhile, farm acreage in 1935 amounted to 308,529.

27. Shreveport *Journal* (centennial edition), June 27, 1935.

28. Glen Jeansonne, "Partisan Parson: An Oral History Account of the Louisiana Years of Gerald L. K. Smith," *Louisiana History,* XXIII

Throughout the 1930s, Shreveporters watched the development of Barksdale Field with great enthusiasm. This reflected their fascination with flight and also their pride in having attracted a major military installation. In September, 1941, there came more direct involvement with the nation's preparation for war when the army carried out the "Louisiana maneuvers," the largest exercises of that type that America had ever seen. Nineteen divisions, divided into two armies and supported by planes based at Barksdale, fought one another across western Louisiana before settling into a mock siege of Shreveport. Lieutenant General Walter Krueger's imaginary Third Army, aided by the staff work of Colonel Dwight D. Eisenhower, finally closed the pincers, after having captured the city's waterworks. Earlier, Major General George S. Patton of the Second Army executed a flanking action with his tanks, hoping to catch the Third Army off guard. Referees disallowed the maneuver because Patton had arranged for service stations along the way to refuel his tanks as they drove all night toward the enemy.[29]

By 1942 Shreveport was organized for the real war. The city's population was close to 100,000, and it was an important center for petroleum, agriculture, lumber, window glass, and iron and steel foundry products. Some 16,000 civilians in Caddo Parish registered for civil defense work. Among them were 1,500 people who trained in first aid and 225 who became auxiliary policemen. Citizens opened a

recreation center downtown to entertain servicemen and maintained it with help from the federal government. Several other facilities provided nourishment and entertainment to traveling servicemen as well as to soldiers at Barksdale. People in Shreveport supported eight different bond drives to raise money for the war. Many also turned to cultivating "victory gardens" to help make up for shortages of food.[30]

Defense contracts brought new jobs to the city. J. B. Beaird and Company manufactured heavy shells and other matériel for the War Department. An ordnance plant between Shreveport and Minden employed around 5,000 people by the end of 1942. Most of those working on the assembly line were women. The plant reserved only 400 or so jobs, however, for blacks, and these were limited to unskilled tasks. Barksdale itself had around 4,500 officers and men, along with 400 civilian employees. Before the war, Congress had continued to invest heavily in the base, more than doubling its strength by 1939. Barksdale became a great training center for aviators on their way to dangerous assignments overseas. In 1944 the base also began to train military policemen. Centenary College joined Barksdale as a training institution when it offered a preflight program for cadets. Assigning 750 young men to a class, the college housed these students on the campus of the defunct Dodd College.[31]

Problems of the postwar period confronting Shreveport were familiar to other southern cities. During the depres-

(1982), esp. 149–53; Jeansonne, "Gerald L. K. Smith and the Share Our Wealth Movement," *Red River Valley Historical Review,* III (Summer, 1978), 53–54.

29. G. Patrick Murray, "The Louisiana Maneuvers: Practice for War," *Louisiana History,* XIII (1972), 117–21, 131–33.

30. "Composite Report on Shreveport-Minden," 6, 65–66, 88; Carruth, *Caddo 1000,* pp. 182, 189; Shreveport *Times,* April 4, 1943.

31. "Composite Report on Shreveport-Minden," 13, 16–17, 19; Carruth, *Caddo 1000,* pp. 165, 181–82.

sion and war, city officials delayed capital projects. After the war, this made heavy expenditures necessary to catch up with growth. Returning veterans needed jobs, though the GI Bill permitted many of them to be directed first into colleges and trade schools. Centenary's enrollment jumped accordingly. Consumers also released their pent-up demand for automobiles, washing machines, and other scarce goods. Local developers rushed to build inexpensive houses in new subdivisions to fulfill the dream of home ownership.

Three large natural-gas companies established their headquarters in Shreveport, but certain young leaders complained that the city failed to recruit other industries. The generation that had returned from the war was impatient with complacency, and through civic clubs and other outlets many campaigned for changes.[32] In general, however, business grew during the late 1940s. The city also secured through the help of Congressman Overton Brooks a new Veterans Administration hospital, which was valued at ten million dollars. A great asset for the local economy was Shreveport's extensive rail connections. By the early 1940s, six rail lines served the city: the Kansas City Southern, the Louisiana and Arkansas, the St. Louis and Southwestern, the Southern Pacific, the Illinois Central, and the Texas and Pacific. Shreveport's support of commercial aviation helped to ensure good service to distant cities.

Local political leadership in the late 1940s fell to a capable mayor named Clyde Fant. In 1947 he secured approval for nearly ten million dollars' worth of capital improvements. By then, the idea of city planning enjoyed wider acceptance, though the rugged individualism born of the frontier and nourished during the great oil booms often resisted government intrusion, especially from Washington. In 1950, Shreveporters approved a home-rule charter—the first for any city in the state. Three years later, they saw the beginning of a master plan for the future.[33] Many local leaders, continuing the business progressivism of their fathers, promoted projects to modernize the city and parish. There was even serious discussion of merging Shreveport and its young but growing neighbor across the parish line to the east, Bossier City.

Civil rights for blacks became a national issue under the Truman administration, though attitudes of local whites remained intransigently against desegregation. Local leadership at least recognized the disparity between white and black schools, which were both separate and unequal. In the postwar period the parish embarked on a program to improve the education of black students. The centerpiece for this effort was construction of Booker T. Washington High School.[34] In a speech in 1948, a president of the chamber of commerce declared that more money ($1.5 million) had been spent on the new black high school than on any other public school building in the city. Yet he doubted that northern critics would pay heed. "The people of the South are

32. Interview with Jim Gardner by Bailey Thomson, May 3, 1985. In 1954, at age thirty, Gardner became the city's youngest mayor ever. Before that time, he had been a member of the Legislature. In 1979 he became the first president of the new Shreveport City Council, which was formed following a change in the city's charter.

33. Carruth, *Caddo 1000*, pp. 191–93, 211.
34. For a contemporary discussion of black schools see Roscoe H. White, "The Problem of Negro Education," *Shreveport Magazine*, III (August, 1948), 16.

frequently castigated by the Northern press and by Yankee moralists and fuzzy-minded reformers for our alleged disgraceful neglect and tyrannical oppression of our downtrodden Negro minority," he said. "The journalistic sewerage that flows through the presses of *Collier's*, *Life* and *Time* emphasize what their blind prejudice considers as our sins and deficiencies, but they make little if any effort to discover our virtues. . . . At this moment when our republican institutions are being assailed by outside enemies and inside foes, it would serve the national interest best to avoid sectional differences and incriminations among our own people." [35] His response signaled an intense resistance to an increasing momentum nationwide for civil rights. It also hinted at an extreme anticommunism that would help to provide a rationale for that resistance by whites in Shreveport and its hinterland.

The city saw the decade end with two events that presented a juxtaposition of past and future. The first was a celebration named "Holiday in Dixie," which favorably invoked the Confederate past. The second event was designation of Barksdale as a base for the Strategic Air Command. Here was both a looking backward to the tradition of white supremacy and a looking forward to the Cold War, which would see fighting in Korea and witch-hunts for Communists at home. Within a few years, the implications of these themes would become more pronounced for Shreveport. Pressure would come from extremist right-wing groups and from the local press to present a united front against integration and other ideas considered to be dangerously liberal.

It would take a quarter century for such resistance to play itself out and for Shreveport to throw off its reactionary image. A desire for economic growth, coupled with progress in civil rights, produced pragmatic reforms that broke down many of the old barriers that had made Shreveport one of segregation's most stubborn bastions. Unlike in 1865, when the city finally yielded to Yankee conquerors, no mythology grew up this time about some lost southern cause. If anything, there was concern that in the city's eagerness to identify with the booming Sun Belt, it might sacrifice the gentle style of living and the small-town friendliness that had sustained its people for generations. Here was a wrenching conflict of values that the city's boosters probably never had contemplated.

35. W. Scott Wilkinson, "Wilkinson Reviews Record-Breaking Year," *Shreveport Magazine,* IV (January, 1949), 11–12.

The Pace Quickens

When Matilde Moisant visited Shreveport in 1912, the Shreveport *Journal* described her as a "petite bird-woman" who had earned an international reputation "for handling an airship as if [she were] a little girl playing with her doll." At a time when women could not vote, reporters apparently found it difficult to describe Moisant in language other than that using traditional imagery. Yet, she embodied the new century—one fascinated by speed and novelty. She was the second woman in the United States to earn a pilot's license. On September 24, 1911, she flew her Bleriot-type monoplane to the astonishing height of 1,200 feet. Her exploits made her a celebrity and a curiosity, and her stage became the crude landing fields of America, where she and other members of a flying troupe risked their lives in exhibitions. (Her brother was killed in an accident in New Orleans.)

Moisant and two male companions brought their airplanes to Shreveport for two days of shows at the fairgrounds. On Sunday, March 18, large, excited crowds came to see them, and when her turn came to perform, Moisant roared off in her monoplane. In landing, however, she lost control of the machine, and it turned over. Many who witnessed the accident were horrified, fearing that she might be crushed under the plane's weight. But she leaped uninjured from the cockpit. Later, she inspected the wreckage, and a bystander took this photograph of her.

Community Fair Collection, LSUS Archives. Donated by Mrs. James H. Butler.

By 1925, automobiles belonging to spectators competed for parking space at the fairgrounds' racetrack in Shreveport.

Community Fair Collection, LSUS Archives. Donated by Ernest R. Roberson.

Although roads remained miserably poor, automobiles brought new mobility to people from rural areas and small towns. Here owners line up their cars after church in Dubach, *ca.* 1915.

Community Fair Collection, LSUS Archives. Donated by Stephen A. Glassell.

The automobile gave young people freedom from adult supervision, thus providing a tenor of youthful zest and daring to the age. Many older people condemned this new mobility, arguing that it encouraged dancing at roadhouses and other "promiscuity." ABOVE: These young women participated in Shreveport's Mardi Gras parade of 1912.

RIGHT: Several young people, dressed in costumes, celebrate the signing of the Versailles treaty in 1919. Their car is decorated in red, white, and blue.

General Collection, LSUS Archives. Donated by Bernice P. Cronk.

SHREVEPORT AIRPORT
OPERATED BY
AIRWAY'S CO. INC.

Photograph by Bill Grabill. Shreveport Chamber of Commerce Collection, LSUS Archives.

When Van Lear Leary and E. B. Redline opened the Shreveport Airport on Greenwood Road in August, 1928, they staged a grand air show in which more than a hundred planes participated. It attracted ten thousand people, each paying fifty cents, according to press reports.

Leary, who was an owner of the Shreveport Airways Company, joined Curry Sanders in 1929 in an attempt to set a world record for continuous flight. In a Ryan Brougham airplane, sister ship to Lindbergh's *Spirit of St. Louis,* they remained aloft above Shreveport for 128 hours and 40 minutes, refueling their craft in midair. But they were unable to break the old record.

ABOVE: Sanders, *left,* and Ed Grace stand beside the airplane at the Shreveport Airport in 1929.

Photograph by Bill Grabill. Community Fair Collection, LSUS Archives. Donated by Larry Davis.

Scene in the dining car during the inaugural run of the passenger train *Shreveporter* on December 20, 1928. The train belonged to the Louisiana and Arkansas Railroad. Crowds turned out along the route to welcome the sleek new addition to the line.

Photograph by Bill Grabill. Community Fair Collection, LSUS Archives. Donated by Mrs. Paul Shapiro.

F DUDDINC

NDSCAPE-GARDENER,
EVEPORT-JEWELLA.

Hoyer Family Collection, LSUS Archives. Donated by Charles Tubbs.

Increasing property values in the business district pushed out residences. The downtown entered its golden era as the focal point for the region's commercial and professional activities. LEFT: One senses the downtown's energy and excitement in the photograph of Texas Street, looking west, taken in 1923. In the background the Slattery Building is under construction. The automobile by this time dominated the city's streets. Traffic required a policeman at the intersection, and parking space was hard to find.

ABOVE: Shreveporters buy fresh vegetables at a farmers' market on the Texas Street side of the courthouse square in 1916.

Photograph by Bill Grabill. General Collection, LSUS Archives.

One street over from Texas, Milam had lost its residential flavor by 1925. For many, Milam's retail stores, lavish movie theater, and city hall made the street the heart of Shreveport's downtown. By the 1920s the automobile had reduced dependence on streetcars, permitting people to live in suburbs farther and farther from the central business district. Eventually, this development ended the downtown's golden era.

Shreveport Chamber of Commerce Collection, LSUS Archives. Donated by Janis Chopin.

In the sales department of Elliott Electric Company in Shreveport, a sign advises employees, DO IT NOW. The year is 1918.

134

Shreveport Chamber of Commerce Collection, LSUS Archives. Donated by Janis Chopin.

The Youree Hotel opened on January 15, 1914, as Shreveport's finest hotel. As a publicity stunt, promoters sent the key to the front door aloft in a balloon, signifying that the hotel would never be closed to customers. Meanwhile a local newspaper hailed the new establishment as another step forward for the city. Here, the staff shows off the hotel's dining room in 1918.

Community Fair Collection, LSUS Archives. Donated by First National Bank, Shreveport.

As business grew, so did the banks in Shreveport. Employees of the accounting department tally figures for the First National Bank, the city's oldest, in 1918.

"Cash and carry stores" pioneered concepts upon which entrepreneurs ultimately would build great chains of supermarkets. By reducing the number of employees and having customers wait on themselves, the stores could slash prices. The Crescent chain had three cash stores in Shreveport when the photographer took this picture in 1918.

Community Fair Collection, LSUS Archives. Donated by Gus Theo.

Theo's Grocery at 607 Texas Street preferred to do business the old-fashioned way, and it lured customers with the promise of fresh fruit. IF YOU DON'T TRADE WITH US, WE BOTH LOSE MONEY, advised a sign in the store. John K. Theo, the proprietor, was a member of the city's Greek community, which grew up after 1900.

So many Italian families lived in Shreveport's Allendale and West End by the 1920s that the sections were known as Little Italy. The Shreveport Italian Band (ABOVE, *ca.* 1920), under the direction of S. Vitale, often represented the Italian community in parades and other public events.

The community also supported an Italian-language newspaper, the *Italia Moderna,* which Standard Printing Company published from its small shop on Western Avenue. The photograph above is from 1929.

SHREVEPORT
La. U.S.A.
AD CLUB

Louisiana State Fair Collection, LSUS Archives.

LEFT: The Shreveport Ad Club's members were active boosters, traveling great distances to promote their city's image. In 1913 in Chicago, members wore derrick hats and dusters to advertise Shreveport's growing importance as a center for production of oil and natural gas.

ABOVE: In 1914 the group helped celebrate the tenth convention of the Associated Ad Clubs of America, which met in Toronto.

Photograph by Bill Grabill. Community Fair Collection, LSUS Archives. Donated by Fredricka Gute.

Community Fair Collection, LSUS Archives. Donated by Mrs. Olin Oden.

LEFT: Christmas at the Doll family's fourteen-room house at the corner of Fannin and McNeil in Shreveport included a formal dinner. Mr. and Mrs. H. F. Doll had nine children. When the family gathered, there had to be room for nearly forty people. The Dolls continued this tradition from about 1925 until 1938.

ABOVE: Members of a wedding party gather in the backyard of Mrs. E. Weldon in Shreveport, *ca.* 1925.

Community Fair Collection, LSUS Archives. Donated by Mrs. Tony Sansone.

Concettina and Grace Brocato of Shreveport in 1918. The nurse's costume no doubt reflects the war.

Community Fair Collection, LSUS Archives. Donated by Mrs. L. H. Crook.

Dorabelle Whitlatch enjoys her toy automobile in Shreveport, *ca.* 1922.

1928

Paul Carriger Collection, LSUS Archives.

Mitchell's Musical Miniatures on the steps of Caddo Parish's new
courthouse in 1928.

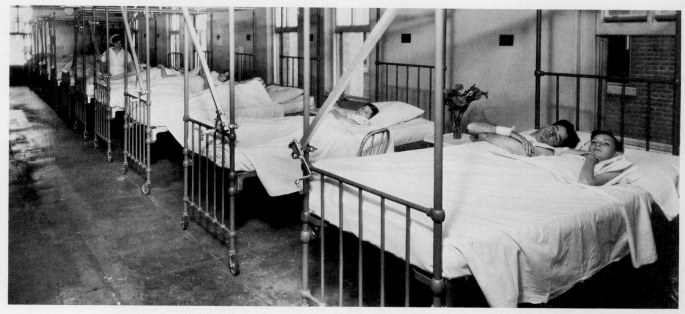

Photograph by Bill Grabill. Gordon W. Maxcy Collection, LSUS Archives.

Improvements in medicine and public health reduced infant mortality and inspired greater awareness of sanitation, proper diet, and control of infectious disease. In 1876 local doctors under the leadership of Dr. James C. Egan reorganized the Shreveport Medical Society. In turn, that group helped to establish a strong state society, to which it contributed five presidents during the next forty years.

One continuing problem the city faced was lack of an adequate hospital for indigent patients. Finally, in 1889 a new Charity Hospital opened its doors to the public. The structure had two floors and sixty-eight beds. It was located on Texas Avenue, on the site of the present city hall. In 1893 Dr. Thomas E. Schumpert became the hospital's superintendent and chief surgeon. He brought about a number of improvements in the hospital, including screens for the windows and an antiseptic operating room. A corps of medical students began training at the institution, which by 1894 was treating on the average 165 patients a month, 72 white and 93 black. By 1902 the average patient load had grown to more than 3,600 annually.

On March 27, 1926, a fire caused severe damage. Afterward, the Legislature appropriated funds to remodel the structure, and the work was finished in the spring of 1929. The photograph above dates from about 1930. Demand for the hospital's services continued to grow. W. K. Henderson, president of Charity's board, declared in the biennial report for 1929–1930: "It is very unfortunate that many deserving patients have to be turned away for lack of room. We have increased the number of beds one-third, bringing the number to 400. This, however, has not relieved the situation as these beds were absorbed by patients who were sleeping on the floors and crowded double in narrow beds. And it has been a source of regrettable criticism from many parts of North Louisiana that patients had to return home without being admitted to the Hospital." In the same report, Dr. E. L. Sanderson, superintendent and chief surgeon, listed recent improvements. For example, food no longer was doled out crudely to patients; each had an individual serving tray. Soap, water, and scrub mops replaced useless disinfectants. And the staff declared war on flies and bedbugs. Patients received fly swatters, and workers sterilized mattresses and repainted bed frames. In 1934 additional wings were built for Charity. Finally, in 1953 the board dedicated a new hospital at Linwood Avenue and Kings Highway. The facility was named Confederate Memorial Hospital.

The rise of powerful medical societies encouraged the growth of the public health movement, and many doctors became crusaders for it. Dr. Egan was president of the Shreveport Board of Health in 1896; two years later, he served as vice president of the Louisiana State Board of Health.

In 1906 the state court of appeals upheld the power of health boards when it permitted the revocation of a license from a milk company in New Orleans that sold impure, adulterated milk. In 1909 the Caddo Parish Board of Health, armed with a new ordinance passed by the Shreveport City Council, reported that it had forced dairies to register and comply with health regulations. To bring the problem of contaminated milk under control was the board's most difficult challenge.

RIGHT: Promoting public health sometimes was a matter of public relations, as was the case with the annual "Better Babies Contest" at the Louisiana State Fair. The photograph shows a doctor examining a contestant in the 1913 contest. In 1915 promoters

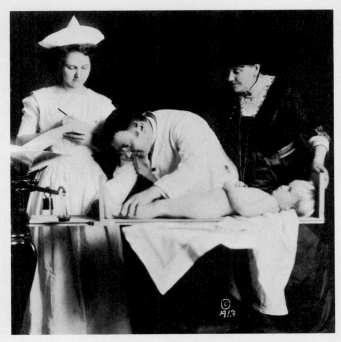

147

Louisiana State Fair Collection, LSUS Archives.

declared that the contest would be scientific. Under the direction of the Child's Welfare Department, the contest became in reality a clinic, in which doctors, dentists, and nurses volunteered to examine children and recommend treatment for physical defects. The idea caught on in hundreds of other cities—a fact commemorated in 1935 with the placement of a tablet at the fairgrounds.

Still, progress was slow. In 1924 the Caddo Board of Health undertook a program to examine school children in the parish. Of 15,591 white children, 7,592 were found to be "defective," according to the Health Board's report. Of 6,700 black children examined, 3,109 were defective. But the Health Board later reported that most of these problems had been corrected.

Hampson Collection, LSUS Archives.

Another public service that became increasingly significant was the Fire Department. RIGHT: In 1910 firemen still depended upon horses to draw their "steamers," but the department had just added its first motorized vehicle.

Hampson Collection, LSUS Archives.

150

On September 4, 1925, a broken water main left Fire Station No. 4 helpless to prevent the spread of Shreveport's worst fire. The flames burned five blocks in the Allendale section and destroyed two hundred houses. A thousand people were left homeless, though there was no loss of life. The Fire Department contained the fire's spread toward the downtown by soaking buildings in the path. The department got water by sending twenty-five empty railroad tank cars to Moore's Station ten miles away.

Photograph by Bill Grabill. General Collection, LSUS Archives. Donated by Caddo Parish School Board.

ABOVE: Increased taxing power enabled the Caddo Parish School Board to undertake an ambitious construction program during the 1920s, which included this new elementary school.

Faculty and students of Ringgold High School for the school year 1917–1918 could all gather on the porch when the photographer visited.

Photograph by Bill Grabill. Webster Fair Collection. Donated by Ann Moore, Webster Parish School Board.

Public efforts to educate black students lagged noticeably behind those to educate whites. The gap was particularly evident in the inferior facilities provided for blacks. Still, segregated black schools instilled in their students a strong sense of community pride. Here students of the Webster Parish Training School for Colored engage in work for drought relief in 1930. In an interview with a reporter for the Shreveport *Journal,* a former student named O. D. Mims recalled how the school's first principal, J. L. Jones, wanted to provide "the opportunity to dream dreams. To dream of becoming lawyers, doctors, college presidents, school principals, teachers, farmers, what have you. . . . Of course, we still carry the belief that there is no reason for failure. We always strive for excellence, the means for survival. We believed it then. We believe it now."

General Collection, LSUS Archives.

Shreveport Chamber of Commerce Collection, LSUS Archives. Donated by Janis Chopin.

William Edenborn organized the Louisiana Railway and Navigation Company in 1903. Known as the Edenborn line, the railroad was the only one in the country owned by an individual. LEFT: A work crew for the company gathers for a group portrait, *ca.* 1920. The boy on the right holding the tools appears eager to claim his place as a laborer.

ABOVE: An office scene in Shreveport shows employees of the same company in 1918. The man in the striped shirt is C. C. Colley, purchasing agent for the railroad.

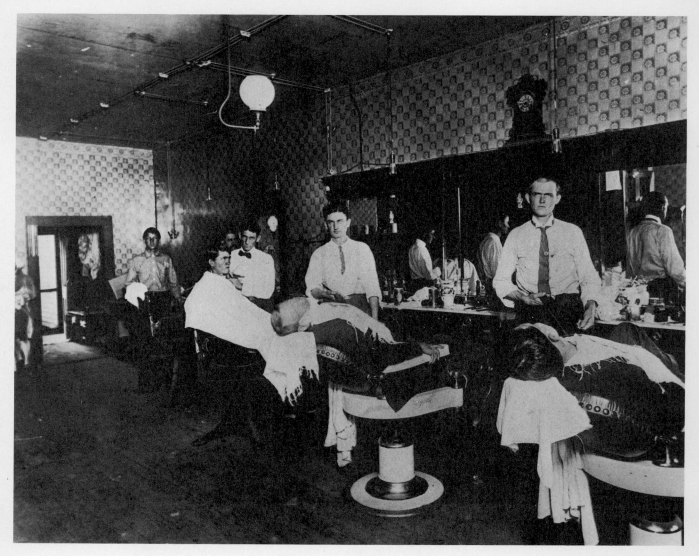

LEFT: Barbers and customers in a barbershop in Vivian, *ca.* 1915.

RIGHT: Sometimes a porch would do. This photograph was probably taken in Caddo Parish. The date is unknown.

Dewey A. Somdal Collection, LSUS Archives.

Shreveport Chamber of Commerce Collection, LSUS Archives. Donated by Janis Chopin.

Customers savored hams from the Cudahy Packing Company in Shreveport. The photograph's date is 1918.

Women sew overalls in the sewing department of Long-Hargrove
Manufacturing Company in 1918. The company's location was
718 Texas Street.

The automobile service department of Crawford-Jenkins-Booth
Company at 201 Crockett Street. The date is 1918.

Photograph by Jeffries & Evans Commercial Photography. Community Fair Collection, LSUS Archives. Donated by Mrs. George Philip Noeth.

Owners and employees of the Shreveport Dressed Beef Company
in the Allendale section of Shreveport. *Ca.* 1914.

Shreveport Chamber of Commerce Collection, LSUS Archives. Courtesy *River Cities* magazine.

Some of Shreveport's early manufacturing companies were in Cedar Grove, which was not annexed by the city until 1926. Among the industries was glass-making, represented in this photo-graph of the B.R.G. Bottling Company at 1 Michigan Avenue. Boys are among the crew making small bottles for pepper sauce. The date is 1918.

Photograph by Bill Grabill. Shreveport Chamber of Commerce Collection, LSUS Archives.

A beauty shop in Shreveport in 1929. Bolder women wore their hair short. Cosmetics were popular, though still suspect.

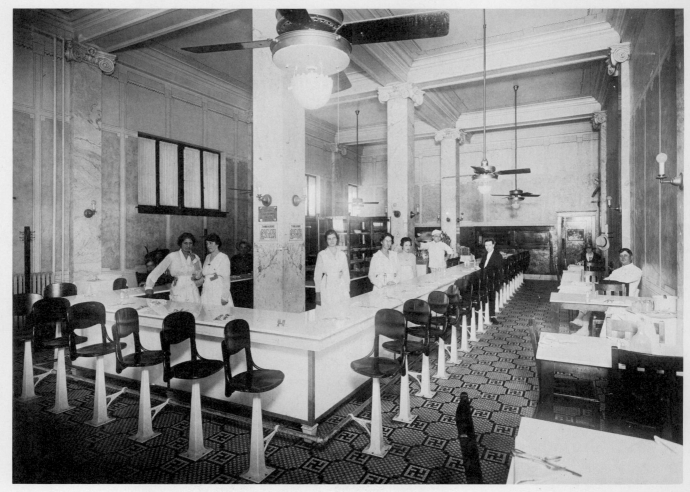

Waitresses attend customers at the Hotel Youree's coffee shop in
Shreveport in 1918.

Shreveport Chamber of Commerce Collection, LSUS Archives. Donated by Janis Chopin.

The Accounting Department of the Wilson Company of Louisiana, a dealer in wholesale meats, at 318–320 Commerce Street. In 1918 the ideal that women should remain at home still prevailed, but reality found increasing numbers of them working.

Shreveport Chamber of Commerce Collection, LSUS Archives. Donated by Ann Clanton.

Foundry Department of the W. K. Henderson Iron Works in Shreveport, 1918. Two years later, the company would mount an intense propaganda campaign against the closed shop.

John Hutchinson Collection, LSUS Archives.

Unions celebrate Labor Day with a parade down Texas Street in 1920. Craft unions were strong, despite widespread but unjustified suspicion that radicalism lay at the heart of the labor movement.

Actually, carpenters, electricians, and skilled workers in other locals tended to be conservative in their outlook and supportive of local civic projects.

Courtesy Hampson Photography and Herbert S. Ford Museum, Homer, Louisiana.

Prospects for growing cotton inspired many people to migrate to Northwest Louisiana. Shreveport's economy depended heavily upon good crops. When prices were bad, both the growers and the businesses that they traded with suffered.

By the 1920s there seemed to be nothing but hard times for cotton farms. Overproduction forced prices down, and boll weevils infested the fields. Here and there in the South, crop diversification met with success, but bumper harvests of cotton oc-

Photograph by Bill Grabill. General Collection, LSUS Archives.

curred in 1925–1926. Meanwhile many of the region's farmers appeared to be sinking slowly into hopeless tenancy. Liens on crops kept many farmers in debt, particularly as prices fell. The crop in 1929 brought less than seventeen cents a pound, down from twenty cents in 1927. When prices fell to six cents or less for the 1931 crop, many tenant families abandoned the land and joined the migration to the cities that occurred during the Great Depression.

LEFT: Wagons crowd around the cotton gin of John Mills Robinson in Homer in 1926. The view looks south down Highway 79. Robinson's gin was one of the first in the area to run on electricity.

ABOVE: Laborers pick cotton on a large plantation in Bossier Parish, *ca.* 1929. The land was part of the twenty-two thousand acres that became the United States Army's Barksdale Field.

Photograph by Bill Grabill. General Collection, LSUS Archives.

Members of an oil-field crew in Bossier Parish, *ca.* 1927.

Discovery of oil in Caddo Parish in 1905 brought Northwest Louisiana into the great oil boom that spread across the southwestern United States. By 1910 the wells in the Caddo Field were pumping more than five million barrels a year. Oilmen even built their derricks on Caddo Lake.

After the opening of the Homer Field, Louisiana moved into third place in production in 1919, behind Texas and Oklahoma. Homer, Haynesville, and other small towns near the oil fields became feverish places, where independent wildcatters competed for drilling rights. Those who were lucky and quick made fortunes. Others went broke just as fast in the mad speculation that followed announcements of new discoveries. Along with crews of roughnecks eager to find work, boom towns also attracted prostitutes, gamblers, and all varieties of swindlers, ready to cash in.

Subsequent discoveries of new fields in East Texas sustained activity in the local oil industry. This meant that many businesses in Shreveport could survive and even prosper during the Great Depression. For many years, veteran oilmen gathered at the curb in front of the old Gardner Hotel on Milam Street to make their deals. Some won or lost millions in "big plays."

Photograph by Sims Lindermann. General Collection, LSUS Archives. Donated by George Doenge.

ABOVE: Jeems Bayou near Stacey's Landing in Caddo Parish, *ca.* 1911.

172

Photograph by Bill Grabill. James Lankford Collection, LSUS Archives.

Along with grime and long hours, oil-field workers faced such hazards as fires. Union organizers enjoyed successes in signing up members, and labor showed its muscle in 1917 when ten thousand oil-field workers in the Southwest went on strike. The union lost that battle, but workers won some important concessions during World War I, including higher wages and an eight-hour day. Depressed conditions after the war, however, forced the workers to accept lower pay again and to go back to working ten and twelve hours. A few more years would pass before the eight-hour day would become the standard for the industry.

ABOVE: Men, mules, and machines on the road to the oil fields in Homer, *ca.* 1919. The muddy street ran in front of the Claiborne Parish Courthouse.

This pipeline crew helped keep the oil flowing to markets, *ca*. 1917.

174

Community Fair Collection, LSUS Archives. Donated by Mrs. J. H. Bentley and Mrs. Julius L. Horton.

ABOVE: Soldiers of Company L, 155th Infantry, at Trees, Louisiana, in 1917. They were present to maintain order during the oilfield strike.

RIGHT: The photographer's caption reads, "No room for the colored man with his cotton patch and cabin." The site probably is the Homer Field in Claiborne Parish around 1919.

NO ROOM FOR THE COLORED MAN WITH HIS COTTEN PATCH AND CABIN

Photograph by Bill Grabill. General Collection, LSUS Archives.

General Collection, LSUS Archives. Courtesy *River Cities* magazine.

Radio

The call letters KWKH, familiar to radio listeners across the country, represented W. K. Henderson's station, which broadcast from Kennonwood, his country place near Shreveport. "Old Man Henderson" (LEFT) projected personality and salesmanship.

Earlier, Henderson, whom one historian has described as "flamboyant and reactionary," had shown an antipathy for labor unions. The W. K. Henderson Iron Works campaigned against the closed shop in 1920, taking out newspaper advertisements that suggested a connection between unionism and bolshevism. Later, through radio, he showed a similar zeal in opposing chain grocery stores. To fight their spread, he organized the Merchants' Minute Men. Money donated to the cause piled up in barrels in his studio, as he relentlessly championed the independent grocers. A shrewd salesman, Henderson seized upon radio's potential to reach customers directly. He pushed his own brand of coffee (ABOVE, *ca.* 1929) and sent a picture of himself along with each order. In 1930 *Radio Digest* declared his station the most powerful in the South.

Henderson sold his interest in KWKH in 1932. In 1935 he took out an ad in the Shreveport *Times* to declare that he was still around: "I have everything I used to have except money," he concluded.

178

Radio's popularity depended, in part, upon broadcasting musical entertainment live from the studios. Two groups who performed regularly in Shreveport were (LEFT) Bert Benton and his Deluxe Night Hawks and (RIGHT) the Pelican Wildcats. Local station KRMD billed the latter as the "Bath Night Entertainers."

Paul Carriger Collection, LSUS Archives.

Photograph by Milburne's Studio. Shreveport Chamber of Commerce Collection, LSUS Archives.

Good Times

Swimming became a form of public-sponsored recreation in Shreveport in 1919 when the city built Victory Natatorium at McNeil and Creswell. Before then, ditches and bayous provided swimming holes for cooling off. One way to draw attention at the pool was to dive from the high platform (LEFT).

RIGHT: These families gathered for an outing and, apparently, some fishing on Black Bayou near Vivian in 1925. The monstrous fish that the man is showing off is a gar.

Jack Norman Collection, LSUS Archives.

Community Fair Collection, LSUS Archives. Donated by Wade Hampton.

Shreveport *Times* Collection, LSUS Archives.

LEFT: The Hirsh Lehman Wampus Cats baseball team, *ca.* 1917.

ABOVE: Shreveport High School's championship basketball team, *ca.* 1915.

ABOVE: The football team of Shreveport High School on Hope Street, *ca.* 1916. High school games began to draw more fans in this era, though the style of play in those years was unspectacular.

RIGHT: Centenary College's football squad in 1921. Despite its small enrollment, the college scheduled games with some of the powerhouses of the Southwest—and often won.

Photograph by Bill Grabill. Shreveport Chamber of Commerce Collection, LSUS Archives.

Photograph by Bill Grabill. Shreveport *Times* Collection, LSUS Archives.

LEFT: Girls' basketball team, Minden High School, 1921.

ABOVE: Lined up for a race in downtown Shreveport, *ca.* 1925.

Photograph by Bill Grabill. Community Fair Collection, LSUS Archives. Donated by Broadmoor Baptist Church.

Evangel Baptist Church in Shreveport, 1930. The congregation later changed its name to Broadmoor Baptist. It grew into one of the largest in Louisiana.

Celia and Ann Sawyer in front of an Ideal Laundry truck in Shreveport, *ca*. 1930.

Helpers for Goodwill Industries in Shreveport serve a meal to transients and poor children, *ca.* 1933.

Photography by Bill Cowen. Bailey Thomson Collection, LSUS Archives.

Sewing room for Goodwill Industries in Shreveport, *ca.* 1933.

Works Progress Administration photograph. Courtesy Louisiana State Library.

The Queensborough Play Center in Shreveport, 1937. The federal
Works Progress Administration organized a number of such pre-
school centers throughout Louisiana.

Federal Extension Service photograph. Courtesy National Archives.

Black 4-H Club members in the community of Bethany in Caddo
Parish enjoy a clothing demonstration in 1933.

4-H Club members demonstrate how to cull poultry in 1933. The community is Shady Grove in Bossier Parish.

Federal Extension Service photograph. Courtesy National Archives.

Members of a 4-H Club in De Soto Parish spray garden vegetables
for insects in 1933.

LEFT: A program sponsored by the federal government's Works Progress Administration (WPA) taught illiterate adults in Caddo Parish to read. This photograph was taken in the late 1930s, probably in Shreveport.

ABOVE: A typical wash day on the Rowland farm at Dubberly in Webster Parish, 1945.

Civilian Conservation Corps photograph. Courtesy National Archives.

LEFT: A member of the Civilian Conservation Corps from a camp in Lincoln Parish holds a welded plow point and a cane-cutting blade that his class made, *ca.* 1936.

The Great Depression saw innovation in Shreveport's public transportation when on July 28, 1931, voters gave the Shreveport Railways Company permission to convert from streetcars to trackless trolleys. The first trolley bus went into service on December 17, 1931. Within eight years, all the old streetcars were gone. RIGHT: Two of the buses glide silently up and down Texas Street, *ca.* 1938.

A teacher instructs her students in a commercial class that the Works Progress Administration sponsored in Shreveport. The year is 1940.

WPA workers in 1942 at the Shreveport Trade School being trained in aviation mechanics and in the construction and maintenance of aircraft.

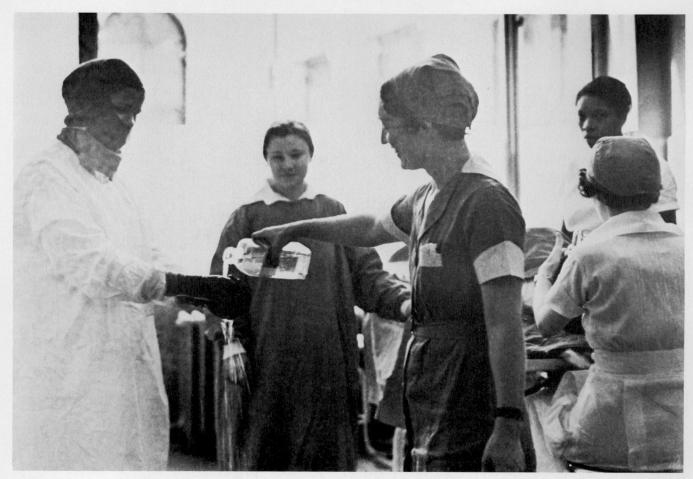

National Youth Administration photograph. Courtesy National Archives.

Young women at work in a laboratory at Shreveport's Charity Hospital, *ca*. 1940. They are participating in a program sponsored by the National Youth Administration.

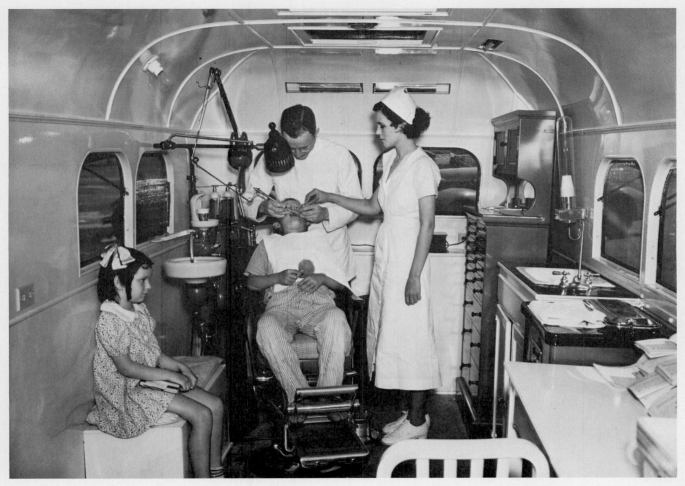

The Public Health Department in Caddo Parish converted a trailer into a traveling dental clinic and used it to treat poor children. Shreveport Mayor Sam Caldwell asserted that the clinic was the first of its kind in the nation. This photograph was made in 1937.

204

Works Progress Administration photograph. Courtesy Louisiana State Library.

Public health officials encountered a high incidence of venereal disease in Caddo Parish. To contend with this problem, they established a VD clinic in the basement of Municipal Auditorium. There was particular concern during World War II that servicemen would become infected; indeed, health officials reported that the rate of disease at Barksdale Field was unusually high for the air corps. The clinic found that venereal disease showed up in 184.9 cases per 1,000 when it examined selectees for the draft from Caddo Parish. Among blacks, the disease was reported to be six times more prevalent than among whites.

Prostitution received much of the blame. Despite an ordinance approved in 1917 to shut down Shreveport's vice district, the practice apparently still flourished, and a new "segregated district" sprang up illegally in St. Paul's Bottoms. Law officers closed it down in 1941. Until then, the venereal disease clinic inspected almost 200 prostitutes each week. Afterward, an estimated 400 prostitutes continued to work clandestinely in the area, and Mayor Sam Caldwell pushed for more repression. The lure of quick profits during wartime, however, made such efforts difficult.

In these photographs, workers from the Works Progress Administration assist in the venereal disease laboratory in 1942.

General Collection, LSUS Archives. Courtesy Barksdale Museum, 8AF Historian Archives.

General Collection, LSUS Archives. Courtesy Barksdale Museum, 8AF Historian Archives.

LEFT: Born amidst cotton farms and dedicated in 1933, the United States Army's Barksdale Field had a look of permanence when this photograph was taken around 1940. Congress had more than doubled the base's strength, and the coming of the war would further intensify activity.

ABOVE: A squadron of A-17s fly in formation over Barksdale Field in 1936.

Works Progress Administration photograph. Courtesy Louisiana State Library.

Soldiers relax at a recreational center in downtown Shreveport in 1941. Local citizens maintained the facility with the help of recreational leaders supplied by the federal government. Later a new USO facility in Princess Park replaced the center.

Works Progress Administration photograph. Courtesy Louisiana State Library.

Officers in the army air corps learn Spanish in 1941 in an adult education project that the Works Progress Administration established at Barksdale Field. The idea was to emphasize the close relationship between the United States and Latin America. Other educational opportunities for military personnel at Barksdale included classes at Centenary College.

Photograph by Doug Perry. Jack Barham Collection, LSUS Archives.

With so many men away in the services, women entered the labor market in greater numbers during World War II. This woman worked for the Southern Switch and Signal Company in Shreveport. The year is 1945.

Photograph by Doug Perry. Jack Barham Collection, LSUS Archives.

Men and mules work in a "victory garden" sponsored by the Southwestern Gas and Electric Company in 1944. Such gardens helped put food on dinner tables during the war.

Photograph by Doug Perry. Jack Barham Collection, LSUS Archives.

Wartime found churches working to keep morale high at home. Dr. M. E. Dodd, shown above in 1944, was pastor of the First Baptist Church in Shreveport. One of the first preachers to broadcast his sermons on radio, he was widely influential among Southern Baptists.

Photograph by Doug Perry. Jack Barham Collection, LSUS Archives.

Drinking coffee at the Columbia Restaurant in 1944. The restaurant was a popular place in downtown Shreveport to swap news and gossip.

Photograph by Doug Perry. Jack Barham Collection, LSUS Archives.

LEFT: ROOSEVELT DEAD says the headline for the Shreveport *Journal*'s extra edition of April 12, 1945. On the left is Douglas Attaway, Jr., managing editor and later publisher. The other man is unidentified.

RIGHT: President Truman's announcement that the Japanese had surrendered led to a spontaneous celebration in downtown Shreveport on August 14, 1945. Cars jammed the streets, and happy servicemen kissed women. Here a soldier holds up the afternoon newspaper that announced WAR IS OVER, while other people mill around in the background.

Photograph by Doug Perry. Jack Barham Collection, LSUS Archives.

Photograph by Jack Barham. Jack Barham Collection, LSUS Archives.

The postwar period found Shreveport's cultural aspirations broadening. A group began organizing a community symphony orchestra in 1947. They met a number of disappointments before they were able to hire John Shenaut as the first conductor the following year. ABOVE: Musicians practicing for a performance in 1949.

Photograph by Doug Perry. Jack Barham Collection, LSUS Archives.

"Vet's Villa" was what people called the typical spartan quarters that Centenary College provided veterans and their families. Like many other colleges, Centenary found itself overwhelmed by the number of returning veterans, who were eligible for the GI Bill and eager to continue their education.

Shreveport *Journal* photograph. Jack Barham Collection, LSUS Archives.

Shreveport claimed two popular politicians in Mayor Clyde Fant, *right,* and Governor Jimmie Davis, shown here in 1946. Davis once served on the city commission. He also had a successful career as a singer and movie star.

Photograph by Doug Perry. Jack Barham Collection, LSUS Archives.

Children in Shreveport memorize Bible verses in 1945 as part of a program to promote "a good Bible memory." The previous year, Dr. N. A. Woychuk, pastor of the city's Cumberland Presbyterian Church, had the idea of sponsoring contests to encourage young people to learn scripture. Within four years, 8,175 youngsters in nineteen states were competing for such prizes as reference Bibles, subscriptions to a Christian magazine, and camping trips.

220

Photograph by Doug Perry. General Collection, LSUS Archives. Courtesy *River Cities* magazine.

By 1949 most of Shreveport's oilmen preferred to work their deals from air-conditioned offices, but a few of the old-timers continued the tradition of trading on the curb market in front of the Gardner Hotel on Milam Street. From there and from the hotel's lobby, traders transacted enough business to make the curb market the largest of its kind in the South.

Soil Conservation Service photograph. Courtesy National Archives.

Migration from the farms continued during the 1940s, as many returning servicemen sought opportunities elsewhere. Much of the area's marginally productive land was converted to timber, particularly following more widespread use of a process for making paper from pine pulp. Thus, the problem of tenant farming, which had trapped families in poverty, diminished. Many who did stay on the farm practiced scientific agriculture and welcomed the federal government's efforts to stabilize prices. A photographer for the Soil Conservation Service in Webster Parish used the Moncrief family in nearby Lincoln Parish to illustrate the bountiful good life that careful farming practices could yield. The year is about 1948.

Photograph by Graham's Studio. Don Graham Collection, LSUS Archives.

Young men dressed as Confederate soldiers pass in review during
Shreveport's first "Holiday in Dixie" celebration in 1949.

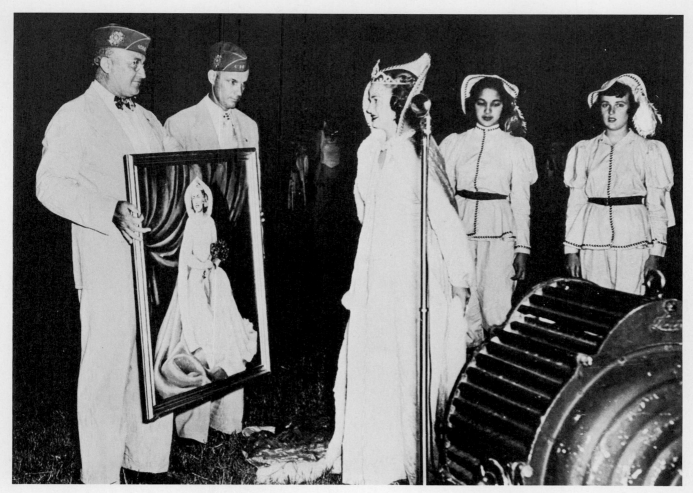

Photograph by Graham's Studio. Don Graham Collection, LSUS Archives.

The queen of the 1949 Holiday in Dixie celebration, Vettye Bern-
hardt, receives her portrait.

A square dance at the Municipal Auditorium in Shreveport in 1949
provides entertainment for participants and spectators.

Bibliography of the History of Shreveport and Northwest Louisiana

Primary Sources

BOOKS AND ARTICLES

Anderson, John Q., ed. *Brokenburn: The Journal of Kate Stone, 1861–1868*. Baton Rouge, 1972.

Bartlett, Napier. *Military Record of Louisiana*. Baton Rouge, 1964.

Bethel, Elizabeth, Sara Dunlap, and Lucille Pendell, comps. *Preliminary Checklist of the Records of the Bureau of Refugees, Freedmen and Abandoned Lands*. N.p., 1946.

Blessington, Joseph P. *The Campaigns of Walker's Texas Division: By a Private Soldier*. New York, 1875.

Brinkley, Floyd O. *Memoirs of a Country Doctor*. N.p., [1947].

Brown, Norman D., ed. *Journal to Pleasant Hill: The Civil War Letters of Captain Elijah P. Petty, Walker's Texas Division, C.S.A.* San Antonio, 1982.

Dimick, Howard T. "Visits of Josiah Gregg to Louisiana, 1841–1847." *Louisiana Historical Quarterly*, XXIX (1946), 5–13.

Dorsey, Mrs. Sarah Anne. *Recollections of Henry Watkins Allen, Brigadier-General, Confederate States Army, Ex-Governor of Louisiana*. New York, 1866.

Fulton, Maurice Garland, ed. *Diary and Letters of Josiah Gregg*. 2 vols. Norman, 1941, 1944.

Hutchinson, Eloise Paxton. *Out of the Past: A Tale of Two Modern Cities, Little Rock–Shreveport*. Shreveport, 1943.

Lloyd, Ben F. *Tandy Key Giddens: An Appreciation*. Shreveport, 1929.

Long, Stephen Harriman. *Report on the Improvement of Red River*. Marietta, Ga., 1841.

Longino, Luther. *Thoughts, Visions and Sketches of North Louisiana*. Minden, La., 1930.

McCants, Dorothea Olga. *With Valor They Serve*. Baton Rouge, 1975.

McCants, Dorothea Olga, trans. *They Came to Louisiana: Letters of a Catholic Mission, 1854–1882*. Baton Rouge, 1970.

Rand-McNally Indexed County and Township Pocket Map and Shippers' Guide of Louisiana. Chicago, 1913.

Red River Line: List of Landings on Red River, November 1st, 1902. New Orleans, 1902.

Sanders, H. C. *The Memoirs of a County Agent*. Baton Rouge, 1983.

Shreveport Blue Book. Shreveport, 1950.

Shreveport Centennial, 1835–1935: Commemorating 100

Years of Progress. Shreveport, 1967.

Shreveport Grange Association. *Address of the Executive Committee of Shreveport Grange Association, to the American People in General and to the Various States of Europe in Particular.* N.p., [1866?].

Shreveport of To-Day. Shreveport, 1904.

Sibley, John. *An Account of the Red River and Country Adjacent.* N.p., 1805.

Taylor, Richard. *Destruction and Reconstruction: Personal Experiences of the Late War.* Edited by Richard B. Harwell. New York, 1955.

Tunnard, William H. *A Southern Record: The History of the Third Regiment, Louisiana Infantry.* Baton Rouge, 1866.

PUBLIC DOCUMENTS

Caddo-Bossier Council of Local Governments. *Historic Sites Inventory and Plan: A Survey of Historical and Architectural Landmarks in Caddo and Bossier Parishes.* Shreveport, 1973.

Freeman, Thomas. *An Account of the Red River in Louisiana, Drawn Up from the Returns of Messrs. Freeman & Custis to the War Office of the U.S., Who Explored the Same in the Year 1806.* Washington, D.C., 1806.

Fullilove, S. C. *Ordinances (1839–1909) of the City of Shreveport, Louisiana, Compiled By Authority of the City Council.* Shreveport, 1909.

Harris, G. D. *Oil and Gas in Louisiana, with a Brief Summary of Their Occurrence in Adjacent States.* United States Geological Survey Bulletin 429. Washington, D.C., 1910.

Herold et al. v. *Caddo Parish Board of School Directors et al.* 136 La. 1034 (1915).

House Documents. 20th Cong., 1st Sess., No. 11.

———. 27th Cong., 2nd Sess., No. 25.

———. 61st Cong., 2nd Sess., No. 680.

Houston E. and W. Texas Railway Co. v. *U.S.* 234 U.S. 342 (1914).

Louisiana. Board of Health. *Report.* New Orleans, 1857–1919.

Louisiana. Board of State Engineers. *Navigation in Red River: Report Submitted by the Board of State Engineers of Louisiana to the Board of Engineers for Rivers and Harbors.* New Orleans, 1930.

Marcy, Randolph B., and George B. McClellan. *Adventure on Red River: Report on the Exploration of the Headwaters of the Red River.* Norman, 1968.

———. *Exploration of the Red River of Louisiana in the Year 1852.* Washington, D.C., 1854.

Scott, W. W., and Ben K. Stroud. *The Haynesville Oil Field, Claiborne Parish, Louisiana.* Baton Rouge, 1922.

Senate Documents. 38th Cong., 2nd Sess., No. 142.

———. 54th Cong., 1st Sess., No. 101.

Shreveport. *Biennial Report of the Mayor and Commissioners of the City of Shreveport for the Years 1925 and 1926.* N.p., n.d.

———. *City of Shreveport, City Ordinances, from January 11, 1910 to March 12, 1912.* Shreveport, 1912.

———. *Ordinances of the City of Shreveport, Compiled and Published by Authority of the City Council.* Shreveport, 1902.

———. *The Plan of Government of the City of Shreveport: Charter of the City of Shreveport, 1950.* Shreveport, 1950.

Shreveport Charity Hospital. *Report of the Shreveport Charity Hospital for the Biennial Period 1924–25*. Shreveport, n.d.

―――. *Report of the Shreveport Charity Hospital for the Biennial Period 1932–33*. Shreveport, n.d.

―――. *Report of the Shreveport Charity Hospital for the Biennial Period 1934–35*. Shreveport, n.d.

―――. *Report of the Shreveport Charity Hospital for the Biennial Period 1936–37*. Shreveport, n.d.

Talfor, R. B. *Photographic Views of Red River Raft Made in April and May, 1873, Under the Direction of C. W. Howell and F. A. Woodruff, to Accompany Their Annual Report on Operations for the Removal of the Raft During the Year Ending June 30th, 1873*. Washington, D.C., 1873.

U.S. Army. Corps of Engineers. *Review of Reports on Red River and Tributaries: Louisiana, Arkansas, Oklahoma and Texas Below Fulton, Arkansas*. New Orleans, 1948.

U.S. Office of Defense, Health and Welfare Sources, Region X, San Antonio, Texas, and National Planning Board, Region V, Dallas, Texas. "Composite Report on Shreveport-Minden, Louisiana War Production Area: Caddo, Bossier, and Webster Parishes." 1942. Copy in LSUS Archives.

NEWSPAPERS

Arcadia *Bienville Democrat*, 1912–72.

Bellevue *Bossier Times*, 1858.

Benton *Bossier Banner Progress*, 1859–.

Blackburn's Homer Iliad, ca. 1860–75.

Bossier Press, 1928–.

Coushatta *Citizen*, 1871–72.

Haynesville *News*, 1910–.

Homer *Guardian Journal*, 1890–.

Homer *Louisiana Weekly Journal*, 1886–90.

Mansfield *Democrat Journal*, 1892–96.

Mansfield *Enterprise*, 1906–.

Mansfield *Journal*, 1891–92, 1896–1908.

Minden *Herald*, 1929–66.

Minden *Press*, 1946–66.

Minden *Press Herald*, 1966–.

Minden *Signal Tribune*, 1929–36.

Minden *Webster Review*, 1935–37.

Minden *Webster Review and Signal Tribune*, 1937–50.

Natchitoches *Democratic Review*, 1885–88.

Natchitoches *Enterprise*, 1888–1965.

Natchitoches *Louisiana Populist*, 1894–99.

Natchitoches *People's Vindicator*, 1874–83.

Natchitoches *Spectator*, 1867–68.

Natchitoches *Times*, 1903–.

Semi-Weekly Natchitoches Times, 1864–72.

Shreveport *Afro-American*, ca. 1920–32.

Shreveport *Bulletin*, 1870.

Shreveport *Caddo Free Press*, 1839.

Shreveport *Caddo Gazette*, 1934–35.

Shreveport *Caddo Gazette* and *Caddo Gazette and De Soto Intelligencer*, 1841–69.

Shreveport *Caucasian, Daily Caucasian*, and *Weekly Caucasian*, 1889–ca. 1913.

Shreveport *Cedar Grove News*, 1927, 1936–78.

Shreveport *Daily Democrat*, ca. 1880–84.

Shreveport *Daily News, Weekly News*, and *Semi-Weekly News*, 1861–66.

Shreveport *Daily Southwestern Telegram* and *Weekly South-western Telegram, ca.* 1852–74.

Shreveport *Daily Standard* and *Evening Standard,* 1878–83.

Shreveport *Herald,* 1896–97.

Shreveport *Italia Moderna,* 1929–32.

Shreveport *Journal,* 1848.

Shreveport *Journal, Evening Judge, Weekly Judge, Sunday Judge,* and *Evening Journal,* 1895–.

Shreveport *Maury's Magazine,* 1915.

Shreveport *News,* 1858–70.

Shreveport *News Record,* 1932– *ca.* 1946.

Shreveport *Progress, Daily Progress,* and *Weekly Progress,* 1892–1900.

Shreveport *Southwestern, Daily Southwestern,* and *Weekly Southwestern,* 1852–72.

Shreveport *Sun,* 1921–.

Shreveport *Times* and *Weekly Times,* 1871–.

Shreveport *Weekly Judge,* 1897.

Sparta *Bienville Messenger,* 1865–66.

Springhill *News Journal,* 1937–52.

Springhill *Press and News Journal,* 1951–.

Vivian *Caddo Citizen,* 1930–.

Secondary Sources

BOOKS

Acker, Jud. *Shreveport Sketch Book.* Shreveport, 1946.

Arnold, Donnis, ed. *St. Paul's Bottoms to Ledbetter Heights: A Succession of Changing Attitudes.* Shreveport, 1985.

Baudier, Roger. *The Catholic Church in Louisiana.* New Orleans, 1939.

Bell, B. Charles., comp. *Presbyterianism in North Louisiana to 1929.* N.p., 1930.

Biographical and Historical Memoirs of Northwest Louisiana. Nashville, 1890.

B'Nai Zion: One Hundred Years. Shreveport, [1970?].

Boisseau, Nettie P. *Record of Oakland Cemetery.* Shreveport, 1940.

Bolinger, Margaret Ann, ed. *S. H. Bolinger & Co., Ltd., 1898–1973.* Shreveport, 1973.

Bragg, Jefferson Davis. *Louisiana in the Confederacy.* Baton Rouge, 1941.

Brasher, Mabel. *Louisiana: A Study of the State.* Richmond, 1929.

Buckner, Zeak M. *The Selber Story.* Shreveport, 1964.

Campbell, Randolph B. *A Southern Community in Crisis: Harrison County, Texas, 1850–1880.* Austin, 1983.

Carruth, Viola. *Caddo 1000: A History of the Shreveport Area from the Time of the Caddo Indians to the 1970s.* Shreveport, 1970.

Caskey, Willie Malvin. *Secession and Restoration in Louisiana.* New York, 1970.

Cassidy, Vincent H., and Amos E. Simpson. *Henry Watkins Allen of Louisiana.* Baton Rouge, 1964.

Caylor, John, and Marion Thurmond. *History of Highland Baptist Church, Shreveport, Louisiana, 1916–1966.* Shreveport, 1966.

Claiborne Parish Sketches. Homer, La., 1956.

Clepper, Lawrence Dixon. *A History of the Republican Party in Louisiana.* Baton Rouge, 1963.

Conrad, Glenn R., ed. *Readings in Louisiana History.* New Orleans, 1978.

Coulter, Ellis Merton. *The South During Reconstruction, 1865–1877.* Baton Rouge, 1947.

Davis, Edwin Adams. *Louisiana: A Narrative History.* Baton Rouge, 1965.

———. *The Story of Louisiana.* 4 vols. New Orleans, 1960–63.

Davis, Edwin Adams, ed. *The Rivers and Bayous of Louisiana.* Baton Rouge, 1968.

Davis, Edwin Adams, Raleigh A. Suarez, and Joe Gray Taylor. *Louisiana: The Pelican State.* Rev. ed. Baton Rouge, 1985.

Davis, Ellis Arthur. *The Historical Encyclopedia of Louisiana.* 2 vols. N.p., [1937?].

Davis, Hester A. *Red River Basin.* Fayetteville, Ark., 1967.

Department of Architecture, Louisiana Polytechnic Institute. *Historical Report: Hollywood House, 2910 Southern Avenue, Shreveport, Louisiana.* Ruston, La., 1984.

Dorsey, Florence L. *Master of the Mississippi: Henry Shreve and the Conquest of the Mississippi.* Boston, 1941.

Duffy, John, ed. *The Rudolph Matas History of Medicine in Louisiana.* Vol. II of 2 vols. Baton Rouge, 1962.

Dunning, William Archibald. *Reconstruction: Political and Economic, 1865–1877.* New York, 1962.

Ficklen, John Rose. *History of Reconstruction in Louisiana, Through 1868.* 1910; rpr. Gloucester, Mass., 1966.

Fineran, John Kingston. *The Career of a Tinpot Napoleon: A Political Biography of Huey P. Long.* New Orleans, 1932.

Fletcher, Mary Frances, and Ralph L. Ropp, eds. *Lincoln Parish History.* Marceline, Mo., [1976].

Ford, James Alfred. *Poverty Point: A Late Archaic Site in Louisiana.* New York, 1956.

Fortier, Alcée. *A History of Louisiana.* 4 vols. New York, 1904.

Fortier, James Joseph Alcée. *Carpet-Bag Misrule in Louisiana.* New Orleans, 1938.

Franks, Kenny Arthur. *Early Louisiana and Arkansas Oil: A Photographic History 1901–1916.* College Station, Tex., 1982.

Gilley, B. H., ed. *North Louisiana: Essays on the Region and Its History to 1865.* Ruston, La., 1984.

Gleason, Mildred. *Caddo: A Survey of the Caddo Indians in Northeast Texas and Marion County 1541–1840.* Jefferson, Tex., 1981.

Gould, Emerson W. *Fifty Years on the Mississippi; or, Gould's History of River Navigation.* St. Louis, 1889.

Goza, Fred E. *Sketchbook of Historic Shreveport.* Bossier City, La., 1977.

Gremillion, J. B. *The Journal of a Southern Pastor.* Chicago, 1957.

Guardia, John Edward. *Some Results of the Log Jam in the Red River.* Philadelphia, 1933.

Gute, Fredricka Doll, and Katherine Brash Jeter. *Historical Profile: Shreveport, 1850.* Shreveport, 1982.

Hair, William Ivy. *Bourbonism and Agrarian Protest: Louisiana Politics, 1877–1900.* Baton Rouge, 1969.

Haley, Gladys Murphy, and Sue Hefley, eds. *Claiborne Parish Sketches*. Homer, La., 1956.

Hardin, J. Fair. *Northwestern Louisiana: A History of the Watershed of the Red River, 1714–1937*. Shreveport, [1938].

Harrington, Fred Harvey. *Fighting Politician: Major General N. P. Banks*. Philadelphia, 1948.

Harris, D. W., and B. M. Hulse, comps. *The History of Claiborne Parish, Louisiana, from Its Incorporation in 1828 to the Close of the Year 1885*. New Orleans, 1886.

Harris, G. D. *Oil and Gas in Northwestern Louisiana*. Baton Rouge, 1909.

Hays, M. S. *Sketches of Old Ruston, Louisiana*. N.p., 1976.

Hefley, Sue, ed. *Historic Claiborne '65*. Homer, La., 1965.

———. *Historic Claiborne '69*. Homer, La., 1969.

Hennick, Louis C., and E. Harper Charlton. *Louisiana: Its Streets and Interurban Railways*. Shreveport, 1962–[1965].

Henrici, Holice H. *Shreveport Saga*. Shreveport, 1977.

Hewitt, Louise Matthews. *Days of Building: History of a Jewish Community*. Shreveport, 1965.

Hilburn, Wiley, Jr. *Reflections of North Louisiana: An Editorial Collection from the Files of the Shreveport* Times. Shreveport, 1978.

The History of Barksdale Air Force Base. N.p., 1971.

Huber, Leonard Victor. *Louisiana: A Pictorial History*. New York, [1975].

Hughes, Jack Thomas. *Prehistory of the Caddoan-Speaking Tribes*. New York, 1974.

Johnson, Ludwell H. *Red River Campaign: Politics and Cotton in the Civil War*. Baltimore, 1958.

Kerby, Robert Lee. *Kirby Smith's Confederacy: The Trans-Mississippi South, 1863–1865*. New York, 1972.

Kerr, Ed. *The History of Forestry in Louisiana*. Alexandria, La., 1981.

King, Grace Elizabeth, and John R. Ficklen. *A History of Louisiana*. New Orleans, 1905.

Kniffen, Fred B. *Louisiana: Its Land and People*. Baton Rouge, 1968.

Krouse, Rita Moore. *Fragments of a Dream: The Story of Germantown*. Ruston, La., 1962.

Landry, Stuart Omer. *The Caddo Indians: Their History and Culture*. New York, [1980?].

Lonn, Ella. *Reconstruction in Louisiana After 1868*. New York, 1967.

McCall, Edith S. *Conquering the Rivers: Henry Miller Shreve and the Navigation of America's Inland Waterways*. Baton Rouge, 1984.

McClellan, Margaret Hutchinson. *William Joseph Hutchinson and Family of Caspiana Plantation*. Bossier City, La., 1975.

McGinty, Garnie William. *Mary Williams Mims: Teacher, Humanitarian and First Agricultural Extension Sociologist*. [Ruston], 1978.

McKay, Mrs. Arch, and Mrs. A. H. Spellings. *A History of Jefferson, Marion County, Texas: One-Time Gateway of Texas Retains Its Glory in Rush and Hurry of Modern Times, 1836–1936*. N.p., 1936.

McLure, Mary Lilla. *History of Shreveport and Shreveport Builders*. 2 vols. Shreveport, 1937, 1951.

———. *Louisiana Leaders, 1830–1860*. Shreveport, 1935.

Mims, Mary. *The Awakening Community*. New York, 1932.

Mims, Sam. *Oil Is Where You Find It*. Boston, 1940.

Mize, Don, ed. *Shreveport Fire Department 514, Shreveport, Louisiana, 1837–1972*. Shreveport, n.d.

Neely, Lalon Greer. *The Early Settlement of the Shreveport Area*. Natchitoches, La., 1965.

Nell, Arthur Howard. *General Kirby Smith*. Sewanee, Tenn., 1907.

Neuman, Robert W. *Historical Locations of Certain Caddoan Tribes [and] the Caddo Treaty of July 1, 1838*. New York, 1974.

Neville, Alexander White. *The Red River Valley, Then and Now*. Paris, Tex., 1948.

O'Pry, Maude Hearn. *Chronicles of Shreveport*. Shreveport, 1928.

Parks, Joseph Howard. *General Edmund Kirby Smith, C.S.A.* Baton Rouge, 1962.

———. *General Leonidas Polk, C.S.A.: The Fighting Bishop*. Baton Rouge, 1962.

Parsons, Elsie Worthington Clews. *Notes on the Caddo*. Mensha, Wis., 1941.

Plauche, J. V. *A Brief History of Holy Trinity Church, Shreveport, Louisiana, and of the Catholic Church in Northwest Louisiana*. Alexandria, La., 1946.

Presley, James. *Never in Doubt: A History of Delta Drilling Company*. Houston, 1981.

Raymond, Helen Marbury. *Holy Cross Church: Background, Beginnings and Development*. Shreveport, 1972.

Read, Frederick Brent, ed. *Up the Heights of Fame and Fortune*. Cincinnati, 1873.

The Red River: A Historical Perspective. Baton Rouge, 1979.

Reynolds, Terry S. *A Cardinal Necessity: The McNeil Street Pumping Station and the Evolution of the Water Supply System of Shreveport, Louisiana*. [Washington, D.C.], 1980.

Ruffin, Thomas F. *Noel at Seventy, 1906–1976*. Shreveport, 1977.

———. *Shreveport: The Trackless Trolley Years, 1931–65*. Louisville, 1984.

St. Amant, Penrose. *A History of the Presbyterian Church in Louisiana*. New Orleans, 1961.

Saint Ignatius, Sister. *Across Three Centuries: A History of the Congregation of the Daughters of the Cross, 1625–1930*. New York, 1932.

Seeliger, Edward, ed. *Historic Claiborne '77*. Homer, La., 1977.

Shreveport Chamber of Commerce. *The Shreveport Story, 1972*. Shreveport, 1972.

Shreveport Geological Society. *Reference Report on Certain Oil and Gas Fields of North Louisiana, South Arkansas, Mississippi and Alabama*. Shreveport, 1946.

Shreveport Medical Society. *Shreveport Medical Society Centennial History*. Shreveport, 1951.

Shreveport Men and Women Builders . . . Shreveport Biographies. Shreveport, 1931.

Sindler, Allen P. *Huey Long's Louisiana: State Politics, 1920–1952*. Baltimore, 1956.

Southern Methodist Church. *History, Organization and Doctrinal Belief of the Southern Methodist Church*. Shreveport, 1956.

Spiller, Wayne. *Branches from the Flournoy Family Tree*. Seagraves, Tex., 1976.

The Story of Poverty Point, Prehistoric Indian Site of 3000 Years Ago. Baton Rouge, 1961.

Stuck, Goodloe. *Annie McCune: Shreveport Madam.* Baton Rouge, 1981.

Tarpley, Fred. *Jefferson: Riverport to the Southwest.* Austin, 1983.

Taylor, Joe Gray. *Louisiana Reconstructed, 1863–1877.* Baton Rouge, 1974.

Thomson, Bailey, ed. *Historic Shreveport: A Guide.* Shreveport, 1980.

Thompson, William Y. *E. M. Graham: North Louisianian.* Lafayette, La., 1984.

Touchstone, Samuel J. *Herbal and Folk Medicine of Louisiana and Adjacent States, Arkansas, Mississippi, Oklahoma, Texas.* Bossier City, La., 1983.

Trelease, Allen W. *White Terror: The Ku Klux Klan Conspiracy and Southern Reconstruction.* New York, 1971.

Tyson, Carl N. *The Red River in Southwestern History.* Norman, 1981.

Vincent, Charles. *Black Legislators in Louisiana During Reconstruction.* Baton Rouge, 1976.

Waldorf, Dan, Martin Orlick, and Craig Reinarman. *Morphine Maintenance: The Shreveport Clinic, 1919–1923.* Washington, D.C., 1974.

Webb, Clarence H., and Hiram F. Gregory. *The Caddo Indians of Louisiana.* Baton Rouge, 1978.

Webb, Clarence H. *The Poverty Point Culture.* Baton Rouge, 1977.

Welborn, Claude A. *History of the Red River Controversy: The Western Boundary of the Louisiana Purchase.* N.p., 1973.

White, Howard Ashley. *The Freedman's Bureau in Louisiana.* Baton Rouge, 1970.

Who's Who in Louisiana and Mississippi: Biographical Sketches of Prominent Men and Women of Louisiana and Mississippi. New Orleans, 1918.

Williams. T. Harry. *Huey Long.* New York, 1969.

Wingate, Ruby Brown, and Nelda Harrell Fleniken, comps. *De Soto Parish Cemetery Records.* Mansfield, La., 1980.

Winters, John D. *The Civil War in Louisiana.* Baton Rouge, 1963.

Winterton, Mary Moss. *Reflections of a Rivertown.* Shreveport, 1975.

Works Projects Administration. *Louisiana: A Guide to the State.* New York, 1941.

Wyckoff, Donald G. *The Caddoan Cultural Area.* New York, 1974.

ARTICLES

Alwes, Berthold. "The History of the Louisiana State Lottery Company." *Louisiana Historical Quarterly,* XXVII (1944), 964–1118.

Arndt, Karl J. R. "The Genesis of Germantown, Louisiana; or, The Mysterious Past of Louisiana's Mystic, Count De-Leon." *Louisiana Historical Quarterly,* XXIV (1941), 378–433.

Baker, Riley E. "Negro Voter Registration in Louisiana, 1879–1964." *Louisiana Studies,* IV (1965), 332–50.

Baldwin, John T., Jr. "Campaigning with Earl Long." *North Louisiana Historical Association Journal,* VIII (Fall, 1976), 27–30.

Barbour, Kirol. "Slum Clearance in Shreveport During the

Gardner Administration, 1954–1958." *North Louisiana Historical Association Journal,* X (Winter, 1979), 1–6.

Baughman, James P. "The Evolution of Rail-Water Systems of Transportation in the Gulf Southwest, 1836–1890." *Journal of Southern History,* XXXIV (1968), 357–81.

Bennett, Charles O. "Public Education in Bossier Parish, 1852–1930." *North Louisiana Historical Association Journal,* II (Winter, 1971), 48–58.

Binning, F. Wayne. "Carpetbaggers' Triumph: The Louisiana State Election of 1868." *Louisiana History,* XIV (1973), 21–40.

Bridges, Katherine, and J. Mitchell Reames. "The Bayou Pierre Settlement." *Louisiana Studies,* IX (1970), 127–41.

Brown, Don. "Caddo Lake." *Shreveport Magazine,* V (January, 1950), 16, 33.

Buice, David. "Shreveport During the Progressive Era: An Overview." *North Louisiana Historical Association Journal,* XV (Fall, 1984), 145–60.

Cadenhead, J. W., Jr. "The Correspondence of Congressman and Mrs. Roland Jones, Between Shreveport, Louisiana and Washington, D.C." *North Louisiana Historical Association Journal,* VI (Winter, 1975), 45–51.

Calhoun, J. D. "Notes on John Stow, Pioneer Planter of North Louisiana." *North Louisiana Historical Association Journal,* X (Winter, 1979), 36–43.

Cawthon, John Ardis. "Make a Joyful Noise: Selected North Louisiana Musicians." *North Louisiana Historical Association Journal,* IX (Winter, 1978), 29–35.

Childs, David W. "Congressman Joe D. Waggoner: A Study in Political Influence." *North Louisiana Historical Asso-*

ciation Journal, XIII (Fall, 1982), 118–30.

Chrysler, Elizabeth. "Allendale: Root of the North Louisiana Dairy Industry." *North Louisiana Historical Association Journal,* X (Summer, 1979), 99–102.

Cline, Rodney. "Keatchie College." *North Louisiana Historical Association Newsletter,* XIII (Summer, 1968), 15–19.

Colbert, William W., Jr. "William Williams Colbert: Bienville Parish Planter (1807–1890)." *North Louisiana Historical Association Journal,* V (Fall, 1973), 21–24.

Cook, Philip C. "The Lake Bistineau Salt Works and Its Civil War Operations." *North Louisiana Historical Association Journal,* I (Winter, 1970), 1–11.

———. "Mt. Lebanon University in Peace and War." *North Louisiana Historical Association Journal,* IX (Spring, 1978), 55–63.

———. "The Pioneer Preachers of the North Louisiana Hill Country." *North Louisiana Historical Association Journal,* XIV (Winter, 1983), 1–12.

Dethloff, Henry C. "Paddlewheels and Pioneers on Red River, 1815–1915, and the Reminiscences of Captain M. L. Scovell." *Louisiana Studies,* VI (1967), 91–134.

Dixon, Gayle. "Establishment of the Twelve-Year Education System in Caddo Parish." *North Louisiana Historical Association Journal,* XIV (Winter, 1983), 51–56.

Dufour, Charles L. "The Age of Warmouth." *Louisiana History,* VI (1965), 335–64.

Dur, Philip F., and Donn M. Kurtz II. "North-South Cleavages in Louisiana Voting, 1948–1968." *Louisiana Studies,* X (1971), 28–44.

Durusau, Mary. "Blacks Fought Hard for Civil Rights."

Shreveport *Journal,* February 22, 1984.

Estaville, Lawrence E., Jr. "Northern Louisiana's Strategic Railroad: The Vicksburg, Shreveport and Texas in the Civil War." *North Louisiana Historical Association Journal,* IX (Fall, 1978), 177–92.

Flores, Dan L. "Beyond the Great Raft: The Freeman and Custis Exploration of the Red River." *North Louisiana Historical Association Journal,* VIII (1976), 1–18.

Forbes, Gerald. "A History of Caddo Oil and Gas Fields." *Louisiana Historical Quarterly,* XXIX (1946), 59–72.

Gardner, James C. "The History of the Municipal Government of Shreveport: A Review." *North Louisiana Historical Association Journal,* I (Summer, 1970), 1–6.

———. "A History of the Protestant Episcopal Church in Shreveport, Louisiana, 1839–1916." *North Louisiana Historical Association Journal,* IX (Fall, 1978), 193–203.

———. "Was Shreveport Planned?" *Shreveport Magazine,* II (December, 1947), 14, 25.

Gaw, Jerry L. "Refuge in a Hostile White World: The Negro Church in North Louisiana During Reconstruction." *North Louisiana Historical Association Journal,* XI (Fall, 1980), 19–32.

Glover, William B. "A History of the Caddo Indians." *Louisiana Historical Quarterly,* XVIII (1935), 872–946.

Granger, Frank. "Reaction to Change: The Ku Klux Klan in Shreveport, 1920–1929." *North Louisiana Historical Association Journal,* IX (Fall, 1978), 219–27.

Grappe, Bernie. "Francois Grappe—Unique North Louisiana Frontiersman." *North Louisiana Historical Association Journal,* IX (Spring, 1978), 65–70.

Griffith, Emilia Gay. "Louisiana Railroads During the Confederacy, 1861–1865." *North Louisiana Historical Association Newsletter,* VIII (Summer, 1968), 20–32.

Guardia, J. E. "Some Results of the Log Jams in the Red River." *Bulletin of the Geographical Society of Philadelphia,* XXXI (1933), 103–14.

Hair, William I. "Henry J. Hearsey and the Politics of Race." *Louisiana History,* XVII (1976), 393–400.

———. "Plundered Legacy: The Early History of North Louisiana's Oil and Gas Industry." *North Louisiana Historical Association Journal,* VIII (Fall, 1977), 179–83.

Hall, John Whitling. "Geographical Views of Red River Valley, 1873." *North Louisiana Historical Association Journal,* XIII (Fall, 1982), 107–17.

Hanks, Dorothy M. "Shreveport's First Electric Streetcar." *Louisiana Studies,* VII (1968), 179–82.

Hardin, J. Fair. "The First Great River Captain: Henry Miller Shreve." *Louisiana Historical Quarterly,* X (1927), 25–67.

———. "An Interesting Resumé of Red River in Trade and Travel." *Shreveport,* VIII (November, 1927), 4–5, 38–39.

———. "An Outline of Shreveport and Caddo Parish History." *Louisiana Historical Quarterly,* XVIII (1935), 759–871.

Hatch, James R. "A Profile: Life in Ante-Bellum Claiborne Parish." *North Louisiana Historical Association Journal,* I (Winter, 1970), 15–29.

Haymans, Karen. "The Decline of the Steamboat on the Red River." *North Louisiana Historical Association Journal,* VIII (Winter, 1977), 77–80.

Hollenshead, Diane. "Central: School Gave Blacks a Chance for Diploma." Shreveport *Journal,* February 22, 1984.

————. "Glory Days of BTW: School Once Featured in *Life* Magazine." Shreveport *Journal,* February 22, 1984.

Honley, Steven Alan. "A History of the 1873 Yellow Fever Epidemic in Shreveport, Louisiana." *North Louisiana Historical Association Journal,* XIII (Spring–Summer, 1982), 90–96.

Howe, J. Ed. "Rettig's Band." *Shreveport Magazine,* II (November, 1947), 32.

Humphrey, Lowin. "A History of Cross Lake, 1883–1926." *North Louisiana Historical Association Journal,* X (Summer, 1979), 85–97.

Humphreys, Hubert. "A History of the Shreveport Carpenters: Local 746." *North Louisiana Historical Association Journal,* XV (Winter, 1984), 1–22.

————. "In a Sense Experimental: The Civilian Conservation Corps in Louisiana, Part I." *Louisiana History,* V (1964), 345–67.

————. "In a Sense Experimental: The Civilian Conservation Corps in Louisiana, Part II." *Louisiana History,* VI (1965), 27–52.

————. "Oral History Research in Louisiana: An Overview." *Louisiana History,* XX (1979), 353–71.

————. "Photographic Views of Red River Raft, 1873." *Louisiana History,* XII (1971), 101–108.

————. "The Red River Raft Briefly Revisited." *North Louisiana Historical Association Journal,* I (Fall, 1969), 10–16.

Hunt, Carolyn. "The Early Schools of Minden." *North Louisiana Historical Association Journal,* IX (Spring, 1978), 97–100.

Jackson, Julia. "Some North Louisiana Delegates to the Constitutional Convention of 1879." *North Louisiana Historical Association Journal,* IV (Spring, 1973), 75–83.

Jeansonne, Glen. "Gerald L. K. Smith and the Share Our Wealth Movement." *Red River Valley Historical Review,* III (Summer, 1978), 52–65.

————. "Partisan Parson: An Oral History Account of the Louisiana Years of Gerald L. K. Smith." *Louisiana History,* XXIII (1982), 149–58.

————. "Racism and Longism in Louisiana: The 1959–60 Gubernatorial Elections." *Louisiana History,* XI (1970), 259–70.

Jennings, Pauline. "Elise Leon: 'First Lady' of the Germantown Colony." *North Louisiana Historical Association Journal,* VIII (Winter, 1977), 43–51.

Jones, Howard J. "Biographical Sketches of Members of the 1868 Louisiana State Senate." *Louisiana History,* XIX (1978), 65–110.

Jones, J. Marshall, Jr. "The History of the Ark-La-Tex Oil Industry." *North Louisiana Historical Association Journal,* XII (Spring–Summer, 1981), 67–77.

Jones, Terry L. "Shreveport Goes to War: Soldiers' Views, 1861–1862." *Louisiana History,* XXV (1984), 391–402.

Krouse, Rita Moore, "Bayou Dauchite: The Ante-Bellum Lifeline of Claiborne Parish." *North Louisiana Historical Association Journal,* II (Winter, 1971), 35–42.

————. "Communication: An Aspect of the Cultural Development of Early Claiborne Parish to 1860." *North Louisiana Historical Association Journal,* IV (Winter, 1973), 42–55.

———. "The Germantown Store." *North Louisiana Historical Association Journal,* VIII (Winter, 1977), 53–64.

Landers, H. L. "Wet Sand and Cotton—Banks Red River Campaign." *Louisiana Historical Quarterly,* XIX (1936), 150–95.

Legan, Marshall Scott. "Railroad Sentiment in North Louisiana in the 1850s." *Louisiana History,* XVII (1976), 125–42.

Lestage, H. Oscar, Jr. "The White League in Louisiana and Its Participation in Reconstruction Riots." *Louisiana Historical Quarterly,* XVIII (1935), 617–95.

Lewis, Wilber H. "Keatchie College." *North Louisiana Historical Association Journal,* IV (Spring, 1973), 96–98.

Lord, Clyde W. "The Mineral Farmers' Institutes and District Fairs." *Louisiana Studies,* X (1971), 92–108.

———. "The Mineral Springs Holiness Camp Meetings." *Louisiana History,* XVI (1975), 257–77.

Lowery, Walter. "Centenary College of Louisiana, 1825–1975." Shreveport *Times,* February 11, 1975.

McCants, Dorothea Olga. "St. Vincent's Celebrates Its Centennial." *Shreveport Magazine,* XXIV (May, 1969), 17, 40–43.

McGinty, Garnie W. "Horse Racing in North Louisiana, 1911–1914." *North Louisiana Historical Association Journal,* III (Fall, 1971), 23–27.

———. "The Human Side of War: Letters Between a Bienville Parish Civil War Soldier and His Wife." *North Louisiana Historical Association Journal,* XIII (Spring–

Summer, 1982), 59–81.

———. "Valuating the Caddo Land Cession of 1835." *Louisiana Studies,* II (1963), 57–73.

McGinty, Garnie W., and Philip C. Cook. "Calvin Leary, 'Model Farmer of North Louisiana,' (1811–1882)." *North Louisiana Historical Association Journal,* II (Fall, 1970), 23–29.

McLaurin, Ann. "The Influenza Epidemic of 1918 in Shreveport." *North Louisiana Historical Association Journal,* XIII (Winter, 1982), 1–14.

Mann, Bob. "Reconstruction Gave Blacks High State Offices." Shreveport *Journal,* February 22, 1984.

Martin, Phil. " 'Leadbelly': A Dangerous Man with a Gift for Singing, Playing the Blues." Shreveport *Journal,* February 22, 1984.

Means, Gay Griffith. "Railroad Consolidation and the Short Line Railroads of Louisiana." *North Louisiana Historical Association Journal,* XIV (Fall, 1982), 157–68.

Miciotto, R. J. "Shreveport's First Major Health Crisis: The Yellow Fever Epidemic of 1873." *North Louisiana Historical Association Journal,* IV (Summer, 1973), 111–18.

Middleton, Stephen E. "Luther Longino, Medical Doctor and Writer." *North Louisiana Historical Association Journal,* VII (Winter, 1976), 49–55.

Mobley, James W. "The Academy Movement in Louisiana." *Louisiana Historical Quarterly,* XXX (1947), 738–978.

Mondy, Robert W. "Societal Evolution of the North Louisiana Frontier." *North Louisiana Historical Association Journal,* I (Summer, 1970), 7–16.

Montgomery, Sally. "The Case of *Herold et al.* v. *Parish Board of School Directors et al.*" *North Louisiana His-*

torical Association Journal, XIV (Fall, 1983), 137–46.

Moore, Waldo W. "C. S. Bell, Union Spy." *North Louisiana Historical Association Newsletter,* V (July, 1965), 13–18.

————. "The Defense of Shreveport—The Confederacy's Last Redoubt." *Military Affairs,* XVII (1953), 72–82.

Morris, Beau. "The Political Origins of Barksdale Air Force Base." *North Louisiana Historical Association Journal,* VIII (Spring, 1977), 131–36.

Murray, G. Patrick. "The Louisiana Maneuvers: Practice for War." *Louisiana History,* XIII (1972), 117–38.

Musselman, Thomas H. "A Crusade for Local Option: Shreveport, 1951–52." *North Louisiana Historical Association Journal,* VI (Winter, 1975), 59–73.

Norgress, Rachael Edna. "The History of Cypress Lumber Industry in Louisiana." *Louisiana Historical Quarterly,* XXX (1947), 979–1059.

Norman, N. Philip. "The Red River of the South." *Louisiana Historical Quarterly,* XXV (1942), 397–535.

Odom, E. Dale. "The Vicksburg, Shreveport and Texas: The Fortunes of a Scalawag Railroad." *Southwestern Social Science Quarterly,* XLIV (1963), 227–85.

Patton, Louise. "The Shreveport Art Club: A Brief History." *North Louisiana Historical Association Journal,* XIII (Winter, 1982), 15–26.

Peoples, Morgan D. " 'Kansas Fever' in North Louisiana." *Louisiana History,* XI (1970), 121–36.

————. " 'Old Hogs and Hominy' Charles Schuler: De Soto Parish Planter and State Public Servant." *North Louisiana Historical Association Journal,* X (Winter, 1979), 19–28.

————. "Seeking a Promised Land for Freedmen: A Decade of Secret Actions by a Shreveport 'Moses,' 1870–1880." *North Louisiana Historical Association Journal,* XI (Winter, 1980), 13–21.

Peoples, Morgan D., ed. "An Excursion Across North Louisiana: Excerpts from the Diary of British Lieutenant Colonel Thomas Fremantle (May 8 to May 15, 1863)." *North Louisiana Historical Association Journal,* VIII (Summer, 1977), 159–69.

Peyton, Rupert. "The Dramatic Saga of the 'Mittie Stephens.' " *North Louisiana Historical Association Journal,* VI (Fall, 1974), 23–26.

————. "Old Shed Road." *Shreveport Magazine,* XVI (March, 1961), 28, 50.

————. "A Webster Parish County Doctor's Record." *North Louisiana Historical Association Journal,* X (Summer, 1979), 103–10.

Pfaff, Caroline S. "Henry Miller Shreve: A Biography." *Louisiana Historical Quarterly,* X (1927), 192–240.

Poe, William A. "North Louisiana Social Life as Reflected in the Ministry of Green W. Hartsfield, 1860–96." *North Louisiana Historical Association Journal,* XII (Winter, 1981), 1–11.

————. "The Story of Friendship and a Book: W. E. Paxton and Green W. Hartsfield." *Louisiana History,* XXII (1981), 167–82.

"Registered Physicians and Surgeons of North Louisiana, January 31, 1886." *North Louisiana Historical Association Journal,* VII (Summer, 1976), 165–75.

Reynolds, Terry S. "Cisterns and Fires: Shreveport, Louisiana, as a Case Study of the Emergence of Public Water

Supply Systems in the South." *Louisiana History,* XXII (1981), 337–67.

Ruffin, Thomas F. "Acadians in North Louisiana." *North Louisiana Historical Association Journal,* V (Fall, 1973), 19–20.

———. "Agrarian Crusade." *Shreveport Magazine,* XXXII (October, 1977), 22–24, 50–52.

———. "Barney Oldfield at the 1910 Fair." *Shreveport Magazine,* XXX (October, 1975), 20, 42–44.

———. "The Birth of Offshore Drilling." *Shreveport Magazine,* XXX (August, 1975), 17–19, 75.

———. "The Bridge That Linked North Louisiana." *North Louisiana Historical Association Journal,* IV (Spring, 1973), 84–89.

———. "Captain Shreve's Tooth Pullers." *Shreveport Magazine,* XXXI (May, 1976), 52, 65–68.

———. "Collapse of the Trans-Mississippi Confederacy." *Shreveport Magazine,* XXX (May, 1975), 22, 36–43.

———. "The Common Man Fights Back." *North Louisiana Historical Association Journal,* VII (Spring, 1976), 91–95.

———. "Decade a Settlement Became a Town." *Shreveport Magazine,* XXVIII (December, 1973), 24, 44–46.

———. "Debt Swamp and How a City Recovered." *Shreveport Magazine,* XXVIII (March, 1973), 20–21, 37–40.

———. "Early Railroading in the Ark-La-Tex." *Shreveport Magazine,* XXV (February, 1970), 18–19, 42–48.

———. "The Elusive Border." *North Louisiana Historical Association Journal,* VIII (Spring, 1977), 95–113.

———. "Fight for Economic Survival." *Shreveport Magazine,* XXXII (November, 1977), 26–28, 41–44.

———. "The Great Raft." *Shreveport Magazine,* XXXI (June, 1976), 20, 65–74.

———. "Invasion of Caddo Parish by General Thomas Jefferson Rusk's Republic of Texas Army, 1838." *North Louisiana Historical Association Journal,* II (Spring, 1971), 71–83.

———. "The Invasion of Shreveport." *Shreveport Magazine,* XXIV (July, 1969), 26, 34–38.

———. "Josiah Gregg and Shreveport During the 1840s." *North Louisiana Historical Association Journal,* IV (Summer, 1973), 141–48.

———. "Louisiana Secession: Northwest Louisiana Convention Delegates." *North Louisiana Historical Association Journal,* III (Winter, 1972), 64–65.

———. "The Mexican Trade Expedition to Shreveport, 1839." *North Louisiana Historical Association Journal,* II (Summer, 1971), 101–109.

———. "Midnight on Ferry Lake." *Shreveport Magazine,* XXXII (February, 1977), 28–30, 50–53.

———. "Origin of Sabine and De Soto Parishes." *North Louisiana Historical Association Journal,* III (Spring, 1972), 94–97.

———. "Premature Victory." *Shreveport Magazine,* XXXIII (April, 1978), 28–30, 60–66.

———. "The Riverboat Comes of Age: Captain Shreve, Part One." *Shreveport Magazine,* XXX (April, 1976), 26–28, 62–65.

———. "Shreve Town." *Shreveport Magazine,* XXXII (March, 1977), 27, 38–42.

———. "Shreveport, 1776–1876." *Shreveport Magazine,* XXXI (July, 1976), 17–22, 42–45.

———. "Shreveport, 1876–1976." *Shreveport Magazine,* XXXI (August, 1976), 28–30, 54–70.

———. "The Textbook Trauma, Part I: The Long Year." *Shreveport Magazine,* XXXIII (August, 1978), 30–32, 72–82.

———. "The Textbook Trauma, Part II: Within or Without." *Shreveport Magazine,* XXXIII (September, 1978), 26–28, 46–53.

———. "The Tragic Trail." *North Louisiana Historical Association Journal,* VII (Fall, 1975), 1–11.

———. "The Year of the Great Epidemic." *Shreveport Magazine,* XXVIII (August, 1973), 34, 52–54.

Russ, William A., Jr. "Disfranchisement in Louisiana (1862–1870)." *Louisiana Historical Quarterly,* XVIII (1935), 557–80.

Sanson, Jerry Purvis. "North Louisiana Press Opinion and the Beginning of World War II." *North Louisiana Historical Association Journal,* XI (Fall, 1980), 33–45.

Schott, Matthew J. "Progressives Against Democracy: Electoral Reform in Louisiana, 1894–1921." *Louisiana History,* XX (1979), 247–60.

Schuler, Kathryn Reinhart. "Women in Public Affairs in Louisiana During Reconstruction." *Louisiana Historical Quarterly,* XIX (1936), 668–750.

Shanabruch, Charles. "The Louisiana Immigration Movement, 1891–1907: An Analysis of Efforts, Attitudes and Opportunities." *Louisiana History,* XVIII (1977), 203–26.

Sherman, Chris. "On the Avenue: Where Black Louisiana Danced Under the Stars." Shreveport *Journal,* February 22, 1984.

Simpson, Amos E., and Vincent Cassidy. "The Wartime Administration of Governor Henry W. Allen." *Louisiana History,* V (1964), 259–70.

Snyder, Perry A. "The Shreveport City Court, Summer, 1873: Presiding, His Honor, Mayor Taylor." *North Louisiana Historical Association Journal,* IV (Fall, 1972), 20–23.

———. "Shreveport, Louisiana, 1861–1865: From Secession to Surrender." *Louisiana Studies,* XI (1972), 50–70.

Snyder, Robert E. "Huey Long and the Cotton Holiday of 1931." *Louisiana History,* XVIII (1977), 133–60.

Stephens, Edwin Lewis. "Education in Louisiana in the Closing Decades of the Nineteenth Century." *Louisiana Historical Quarterly,* XVI (1933), 38–57.

Still, William N. "The Confederate Ironclad *Missouri.*" *Louisiana Studies,* IV (1965), 101–10.

Stuck, Goodloe R. "Log Houses in Northwest Louisiana." *Louisiana Studies,* X (1971), 225–37.

Suarez, Raleigh A. "Bargains, Bills, and Bankruptcies: Business Activity in Rural Antebellum Louisiana." *Louisiana History,* III (1966), 189–206.

"Survey of the Negro Community." *Shreveport Magazine,* VIII (July, 1953), 20–21, 31–32.

Sutherland, Daniel E. "Looking for a Home: Louisiana Emigrants During the Civil War and Reconstruction." *Louisiana History,* XXI (1980), 341–59.

Taylor, Tony. "Touching All the Bases: The History of Integration in Professional Baseball in Shreveport." *North Louisiana Historical Association Journal,* XV (Winter, 1984), 23–29.

Thompson, Alan S. "The Caspiana 'Big House': History

and Restoration." *North Louisiana Historical Association Journal*, XIX, (Summer, 1978), 107–14.

Trudeau, Nancy B. "Sawyer Downs: 'Right Place, Wrong Time.'" *North Louisiana Historical Association Journal*, XIV (Winter, 1983), 41–50.

Tucker, Steve. "The Louisiana Hayride, 1948–1954." *North Louisiana Historical Association Journal*, VIII (Fall, 1977), 187–201.

Tunnell, T. B., Jr. "The Negro, the Republican Party, and the Election of 1876 in Louisiana." *Louisiana History*, VII (1966), 101–16.

Vetter, Eddie. "Henry Adams—Looking For a Way Out." Shreveport *Journal*, February 22, 1984.

Wetta, Frank J. " 'Bulldozing the Scalawags': Some Examples of the Persecution of Southern White Republicans in Louisiana During Reconstruction." *Louisiana History*, XXI (1980), 43–58.

White, Roscoe H. "City Is Outgrowing Its Schools." *Shreveport Magazine*, III (July, 1948), 1–13, 21–27.

———. "The Problem of Negro Education." *Shreveport Magazine*, III (August, 1948), 16–17, 24–29.

Wikstrom, Debbie. "The Horse-Drawn Street Railway: The Beginning of Public Transportation in Shreveport, 1870–1872." *North Louisiana Historical Association Journal*, VII (Spring, 1976), 83–90.

Wilkins, S. A. "Caddo Parish Wants a Junior College." *North Louisiana Historical Association Journal*, XIV (Spring–Summer, 1983), 103–10.

———. "Dodd College: A Brief History." *North Louisiana Historical Association Journal*, XI (Summer, 1980), 29–34.

———. "Dodd College, Shreveport, Louisiana: Northwest Louisiana Junior College of LSU?" *North Louisiana Historical Association Journal*, XIV (Winter, 1983), 13–20.

Wilkinson, W. Scott. "Wilkinson Reviews Record-Breaking Year." *Shreveport Magazine*, IV (January, 1949), 11–12.

Williams, Beverly S. "Anti-Semitism and Shreveport, Louisiana: The Situation in the 1920s." *Louisiana History*, XXI (1980), 387–98.

Wilson, J. Woodfin, Jr. "Some Aspects of Medical Services in the Trans-Mississippi Department of Confederate States of America, 1863–1865." *North Louisiana Historical Association Journal*, XII (Fall, 1981), 123–46.

Windham, William T. "The Problem of Supply in the Trans-Mississippi Confederacy." *Journal of Southern History*, XVII (1961), 149–68.

THESES AND DISSERTATIONS

Barker, Olden Lee. "An Historical Account of the Red River as an Inland Water-way." M.A. thesis, University of Colorado, 1929.

Binning, F. Wayne. "Cooperation and Obstruction in the Louisiana Secession Crisis." M.A. thesis, Louisiana State University, 1965.

———. "Henry Clay Warmouth and Louisiana Reconstruction." Ph.D. dissertation, University of North Carolina, 1969.

Breen, Kermit Townsend. "A History of the Shreveport Symphony Society from 1948–1967." Ph.D. dissertation, Florida State University, 1970.

Brown, Edward Devereaux. "A History of the Shreveport Little Theatre." Ph.D. dissertation, University of Denver, 1958.

Carrigan, Jo Ann. "The Saffron Scourge: A History of Yellow Fever in Louisiana, 1796–1905." Ph.D. dissertation, Louisiana State University, 1961.

Chapman, William D. "Water Transportation in Louisiana, 1862–1877." M.A. thesis, Louisiana State University, 1956.

Covington, Jess Baker. "A History of the Shreveport Times." Ph.D. dissertation, University of Missouri, 1964.

Constantin, Roland Paul. "The Louisiana 'Black Code' Legislation of 1865." M.A. thesis, Louisiana State University, 1956.

Culbertson, Manie (Lyles). "The Caddo Indians." M.E. thesis, Northwestern State College of Louisiana, 1962.

Curry, Lamar Clayton. "Economic Implications of the Red River Raft." M.A. thesis, Louisiana State University, 1939.

Dalrymple, Andrew E. "Business as Usual: Presidential Reconstruction in Caddo Parish, Louisiana." M.A. thesis, University of Houston at Clear Lake City, 1984.

Dawson, Joseph Green, III. "Five Generals in Louisiana Reconstruction, 1865–1868." M.A. thesis, Louisiana State University, 1970.

Dyer, Grace Elizabeth Farmer. "The Removal of the Great Raft in Red River." M.A. thesis, Louisiana State University, 1948.

Ferguson, Ted. "The Louisiana Constitution of 1845." M.A. thesis, Louisiana State University, 1948.

Furrh, Margaret Jean. "Henry Miller Shreve: His Contributions to Navigation on the Western Rivers of the United States." M.A. thesis, Texas Tech University, 1971.

Glover, William Bonny. "A History of the Caddo Indians." M.A. thesis, University of Texas, 1935.

Gonzales, John E. "William Pitt Kellogg, Reconstruction Governor of Louisiana, 1873–1877." M.A. thesis, Louisiana State University, 1945.

Griffin, Emilia Gay. "Building the Texas and Pacific Railway in Louisiana, 1850–1920." M.A. thesis, Northwestern Louisiana University, 1968.

Grosz, Agnes Smith. "The Political Career of Pinckney Benton Stewart Pinchback." M.A. thesis, Louisiana State University, 1943.

Guardia, John Edward. "Successive Adjustments to Raft Conditions in Lower Red River Valley." M.A. thesis, University of Chicago, 1927.

Hall, Lillian Jones. "A Historical Study of Programming Techniques and Practices of Radio Station KWKH, Shreveport, Louisiana, 1922–1950." Ph.D. dissertation, Louisiana State University, 1959.

Harper, Clifton Edward. "The Country Press of Louisiana, 1860–1910." M.A. thesis, Louisiana State University, 1939.

Harper, Myrtle Buckley. "The Country Press of Louisiana, 1794–1860." M.A. thesis, Louisiana State University, 1939.

Heron, Stella. "The Secession Movement in Louisiana, 1850–1861." M.A. thesis, Tulane University, 1913.

Hick, Harold. "The Development of Banking in Louisiana." M.A. thesis, Louisiana State University, 1931.

Highsmith, William E. "Louisiana During Reconstruction." Ph.D. dissertation, Louisiana State University, 1939.

Hyams, Valery G. "A History of Navigation on the Red River, 1815–1865." M.A. thesis, Louisiana State University, 1939.

Kramer, Ethel Elizabeth. "Slavery Legislation in Ante-Bellum Louisiana, 1803–1860." M.A. thesis, Louisiana State University, 1944.

Kyser, John S. "The Evolution of Louisiana Parishes in Relation to Population Growth and Movements." M.A. thesis, Louisiana State University, 1938.

Landry, Thomas R. "The Political Career of Robert Charles Wickliffe." M.A. thesis, Louisiana State University, 1939.

LeBlanc, Doris Mae. "The Development and Growth of the Oil Industry in Caddo Parish." M.A. thesis, Louisiana State University, 1949.

LeBreton, Marietta Marie. "A History of the Factory System Serving the Louisiana Indians." M.A. thesis, Louisiana State University, 1961.

Leland, Edwin Albert. "Organization and Administration of the Louisiana Army During the Civil War." M.A. thesis, Louisiana State University, 1938.

Lindsey, Henry C. "The History of the Theater in Shreveport, Louisiana to 1900." M.A. thesis, Louisiana State University, 1954.

Lowery, Walter McGehee. "The Political Career of James Madison Welles." M.A. thesis, Louisiana State University, 1947.

Marsala, Vincent J. C. "The Louisiana Unification Movement of 1873." M.A. thesis, Louisiana State University, 1962.

Martin, Margaret Ann. "Colonel Robert Ewing, Louisiana Journalist and Politician." M.A. thesis, Louisiana State University, 1964.

McCleish, Dolph W. "Louisiana and the Kansas Question, 1854–1861." M.A. thesis, Louisiana State University, 1962.

McDaniel, Hilda Mulvey. "Francis Tillou Nicholls and the End of Reconstruction." M.A. thesis, Louisiana State University, 1946.

Merrill, John C., Jr. "Louisiana Public Opinion on Secession, 1859–1860." M.A. thesis, Louisiana State University, 1950.

Nichols, C. Howard. "Francis Tillou Nicholls, Bourbon Democrat." M.A. thesis, Louisiana State University, 1959.

Norton, Leslie M. "A History of the Whig Party in Louisiana." Ph.D. dissertation, Louisiana State University, 1940.

Palmer, Frances Hilley. "The Development of the Natural Gas Industry in the Shreveport Area." M.A. thesis, University of Colorado, 1951.

Ricketts, William Boyce. "Exploration of the Southwestern Borders of the Louisiana Purchase, 1803–1807." M.A. thesis, University of California, n.d.

Robert, Mary Elizabeth Phillips. "The Background of Negro Disfranchisement in Louisiana." M.A. thesis, Tulane University, 1932.

Sanders, Gary E. "The Election to the Secession Convention in Louisiana." M.A. thesis, Louisiana State University, 1968.

Schochler, Floy F. "Louisiana Baptists and the War for Southern Independence." M.A. thesis, Louisiana State University, 1958.

Schuler, Kathryn R. "Women in Shreveport During Reconstruction." M.A. thesis, Louisiana State University, 1936.

Scurlock, Jack Daniel. "The Kadohadacho Indians: A Correlation of Archaeological and Documentary Data." M.A. thesis, University of Texas, 1965.

Shoalmire, Jimmie G. "Carpetbagger Extraordinary: Marshall Harvey Twitchell, 1840–1905." Ph.D. dissertation, Mississippi State University, 1969.

Snyder, Perry Anderson. "Shreveport, Louisiana, During the Civil War and Reconstruction." Ph.D. dissertation, Florida State University, 1979.

Updegraff, Donald R. "The Development and Growth of Banking in Shreveport, Louisiana." Special thesis, Rutgers University, 1975.

Weaver, Richard. "The Confederate South, 1865–1910: A Study in the Survival of a Mind and a Culture." Ph.D. dissertation, Louisiana State University, 1943.

Windham, Allie B. "Methods and Mechanisms Used to Restore White Supremacy in Louisiana, 1872–1876." M.A. thesis, Louisiana State University, 1948.

Index